T0277140

# Cambridge Elements ≡

Elements in the Economics of Emerging Markets
edited by
Bruno S. Sergi
*Harvard University*

# ADVANCED ISSUES IN THE GREEN ECONOMY AND SUSTAINABLE DEVELOPMENT IN EMERGING MARKET ECONOMIES

Elena G. Popkova
MGIMO University

CAMBRIDGE
UNIVERSITY PRESS

# CAMBRIDGE
## UNIVERSITY PRESS

University Printing House, Cambridge CB2 8BS, United Kingdom

One Liberty Plaza, 20th Floor, New York, NY 10006, USA

477 Williamstown Road, Port Melbourne, VIC 3207, Australia

314–321, 3rd Floor, Plot 3, Splendor Forum, Jasola District Centre,
New Delhi – 110025, India

103 Penang Road, #05–06/07, Visioncrest Commercial, Singapore 238467

Cambridge University Press is part of the University of Cambridge.

It furthers the University's mission by disseminating knowledge in the pursuit of
education, learning, and research at the highest international levels of excellence.

www.cambridge.org
Information on this title: www.cambridge.org/9781009097987
DOI: 10.1017/9781009093408

First published 2022

*A catalogue record for this publication is available from the British Library.*

ISBN 978-1-009-09798-7 Paperback
ISSN 2631-8598  (online)
ISSN 2631-858X (print)

# Advanced Issues in the Green Economy and Sustainable Development in Emerging Market Economies

Elements in the Economics of Emerging Markets

DOI: 10.1017/9781009093408
First published online: March 2022

Elena G. Popkova
*MGIMO University*

**Author for correspondence:** Elena G. Popkova, elenapopkova@yahoo.com

**Abstract:** This Element goes far beyond economic theory. It will be of interest to representatives of the environmental sciences due to its focus on the 'green' economy and sustainable development. It will also be appealing to representatives of the social sciences, as it takes into account the peculiarities of emerging market economies. Learning from the COVID-19 pandemic and crisis makes this Element interesting from a health economics perspective.

**Keywords:** green economy, sustainable development, emerging market economies, COVID-19, crisis management

ISBNs: 9781009097987 (PB), 9781009093408 (OC)
ISSNs: 2631-8598 (online), 2631-858X (print)

# Contents

Introduction: Green Economy and Sustainable
Development As the Basis for High Performance of
Emerging Market Economies and the Legacy of the
Coming Generations                                                    1

1 The COVID-19 Crisis As a Barrier to the Formation of the
  Green Economy and Sustainable Development in
  Emerging Market Economies                                          6

2 Specific Nature of the Impact of the COVID-19 Crisis on
  Sustainable Development and the Green Economy in
  Emerging Market Economies                                         24

3 The COVID-19 Crisis: Potential Harm to Sustainable
  Development and the Green Economy and Prospects for
  Mitigating It As a New Challenge for State Management            40

4 Scenarios of Sustainable Development of Emerging
  Market Economies amid the COVID-19 Crisis
  and Prospects for the Green Economy's
  Anti-crisis Management                                            56

  Conclusion: Green Economy and Sustainable
  Development amid the COVID-19 Crisis: Looking
  into the Future of Emerging Market Economies                     73

  References                                                        79

# Introduction
## Green Economy and Sustainable Development
## As the Basis for High Performance of Emerging Market Economies and the Legacy of the Coming Generations

Sustainable development is a strategic priority of humanity, the value of which resides in the combination of development as an embodiment of progress – the movement forward to a better future for everyone – and sustainability – the embodiment of stability and harmony between society, economy, and environment. The United Nations (UN) Sustainable Development Goals (SDGs) unified the whole world in the implementation of the global initiative of provision of the well-being of the world's modern population and preservation of heritage for future generations.

Seventeen SDGs give us pause for thought about what we are doing wrong and to what the current economic practices will lead, as well as what we should strive towards to make the world better. The SDGs reflect the true interests of modern times in such a precise way that they have received full support from international organizations, governments, local communities, civil societies, businesses, and all who have not remained indifferent and changed their lives in the interests of peace and prosperity.

The green economy is one of the main mechanisms of the practical implementation of the SDGs, the large potential of which is denoted by the very name of this mechanism, which combines green principles (interests of environment protection) and economic practices. The significance of the green economy is explained by the fact that it allows attaining several SDGs and generates a synergetic effect in the form of support (positive externalities) for the implementation of those SDGs that are not connected to environment protection.

Thus the green economy envisages a transition to affordable and clean energy (SDG7), the creation of sustainable cities and communities (SDG11), and the development and establishment of responsible production and consumption (SDG12). The green economy stimulates the fight against climate change (SDG13) and for the preservation of life below water (SDG14) and on land (SDG15). All this ensures a more favourable environment, with more accessible clean water and sanitation (SDG6), active development of agriculture and liquidation of hunger (SDG2) and poverty (SDG1), improvement of health and well-being (SDG3), and wider possibilities for the development of society and economy, all of which provides a synergetic effect.

This is what differentiates the green economy from other existing mechanisms of implementing the SDGs, most of which generate a positive effect for only one of these goals without influencing the others. For example, the mechanism of social inclusion allows reducing or even fully overcoming gender, cultural (ethnic), and other inequalities but has a small impact on ecology. That is why it is important to develop the green economy: because of its top-priority role in the systemic implementation of the SDGs.

Sustainable development is a symbol of hope for a better world for modern and future generations, the path to which lies through the creation of the green economy. This hope must not die. However, it is seriously threatened by the COVID-19 pandemic, which started in 2020 and continues currently. This threat is unique by its nature; it is new and thus especially dangerous. It should be noted that crises in a market economy are a normal (inevitable and frequent) phenomenon. They are predictable to a certain extent and understandable; they are always followed by a rise which takes economic systems to further progress.

In the late twentieth and early twenty-first centuries, all crises (including political crises) were of a socio-economic nature and opened the doors to new opportunities for growth and development. For example, the dissolution of the Soviet Union in the 1990s was, first of all, a socio-economic transformation, a change of the political system, and a transformation of the cost-creation chains. The Soviet Union was replaced by the Commonwealth of Independent States (CIS) and the Eurasian Economic Union (EAEU).

Similarly, the 2008 financial crisis was caused by the overheating of financial markets. It led to the replacement of financial innovations by high technologies; post-industrial economies that specialized in the service sphere gave way to neo-industrial economies (Industry 4.0) with developed hi-tech industry and dissemination of digital technologies in all economic spheres.

The following (starting in 2014) crisis of the change of the global order (a transition from a unipolar world with the domination of developed countries, to a multipolar world against a background of the intensive growth of emerging market economies) was accompanied by the implementation of international economic sanctions. Against the background of these crises, the COVID-19 pandemic is a stand-alone phenomenon that emerged and developed under the influence of a third (natural, independent from human) power.

Amid the healthcare crisis there are no winners. All countries of the world are losers since the whole of humankind is under mortal threat. From the position of philosophy, the pandemic could be treated as an uprising of nature against the irresponsible use of nature in recent decades. The ecological costs of economic growth have been constantly on the rise while its rate has been increasing as well. An ecological crisis has been brewing for a long time and was openly discussed, but people refused to believe it was imminent. This crisis manifested in a very unexpected way; instead of the most predictable natural disaster, there appeared a new and dangerous infectious disease, resistant to existing medical treatments.

Natural disasters are frequent, such as large forest fires, flooding of cities, anomalous heat and cold, and melting of ice. One of the most probable explanations of the emergence of COVID-19 says that this is a new zoonotic disease which appeared due to the disharmony of society and nature – a critical reduction of biodiversity, ousting of animals from their usual habitat, and transmitting their infections to humans.

The main question that bothers humanity right now is, what damage has the COVID-19 pandemic and crisis caused to sustainable development and what are the prospects of further implementation of the SDGs? The UN justly called the modern period of sustainable development a 'Decade of Action'. It is necessary to act to keep up with the schedule and fully implement all SDGs by 2030. However, a serious obstacle in this path is global inequality (of countries).

Emerging market economies, also called developing countries, face the ecological costs of global economic growth to the largest extent. Having no access to leading technologies, many emerging market economies are forced to specialize in the extraction and export of natural and energy resources. Even support from international organizations does not allow taking developing countries to the same level of social, economic, and technological progress as developed countries; it only insignificantly decreases the gap between these categories of countries.

Sustainable Development Goals are a field in which there is no competition for global leadership among countries. In this field, all countries have to cooperate as partners, jointly implementing the SDGs, especially the ones connected to environmental protection. Ecology is common to the entire planet. That is why, for example, large carbon emissions and the emergence of ozone holes in the territory of developing countries will cause consequences around the world, impacting developed countries as well.

Proof of this is the fact that developed countries with low ecological costs of economic growth and a generally favourable environment faced significant manifestations of climate change in 2020–1. For example, the USA was ranked twenty-fifth in the world by the pollution index in 2021 (39.26 points) and forty-seventh in the world by the climate index (77.49 points). Japan was ranked twenty-fourth in the world by the pollution index in 2021 (39.10 points) and thirty-first in the world by the climate index (85.27 points) (Numbeo, 2021).

Levels of healthcare are much higher in developed countries. Also, developed countries conduct mass vaccination of their populations. Unlike developed countries, developing countries face a deficit of vaccines and large risks of insanitary conditions, causing them to suffer more from the COVID-19 pandemic, and they are slow in dealing with the viral threat. A notable example of this is the increased outbreak of cases in India in the first half of 2021, which led to a high death rate.

All of this highlights the importance of a thorough scientific study of the experience of sustainable development based on the green economy of emerging market economies amid the COVID-19 pandemic and crisis. The purpose of this Element is systemic research of this experience and determination of tendencies, barriers, and prospects, as well as the formation of the scientific and methodological provision and suggestion of the complex applied recommendations for sustainable development based on the green economy of emerging market economies amid the COVID-19 pandemic and crisis.

This Element uses a 'narrow' interpretation of sustainable development – in strict relation to the green economy – and also discusses the relevant SDGs (1–3, 6–7, 11–15). The originality of this Element lies in taking into account the pandemic context and the latest experience in the development of a 'green' economy and the implementation of related SDGs in the context of the COVID-19 crisis. The uniqueness of the Element is that it examines a large sample of developing (including lagging) countries. For this, firstly, sources of statistics have been selected which contain data on a large list of developing countries on the topic of green economy and sustainable development. Secondly, the study is structured in such a way as to use these statistics to form an evidence base.

This Element's audience primarily includes scholars who study the issues of sustainable development, the green economy, and the specifics of emerging market economies. In the Element, they will find answers to the questions regarding the impact of the COVID-19 pandemic and crisis on sustainable development of emerging market economies, as well as leading scientific and methodological developments in the sphere of the COVID-19 crisis management in these countries based on green economy management.

This Element might also be interesting and useful for readers outside of the academic community, mainly state regulators in emerging market economies. For them, the Element offers applied solutions and scientifically substantiated recommendations (ready to be implemented) for the most effective anti-crisis management of sustainable development and accelerated implementation of the SDGs during the 'Decade of Action' based on green economy development.

This Element contains four sections which consecutively demonstrate that the green economy and sustainable development are the basis of high indicators of emerging market economies and the heritage of future generations, demonstrating the challenges they face during the COVID-19 pandemic and crisis. It also explains how to provide an effective reaction to these challenges to successfully implement the SDGs in the period until 2030. The sections contain case studies and the critical analysis of the empirical experience of different emerging market economies.

In Section 1, the COVID-19 crisis is studied in detail and is defined as an obstacle in the path of the formation of the green economy and sustainable development in emerging market economies. It studies the impact of the COVID-19 crisis on the green economy in emerging market economies, considers the case experience (successful examples) of implementing green initiatives in the Russian economy in 2020 amid the COVID-19 crisis, performs factor analysis of the impact of economic levers on implementing the green SDGs in emerging market economies, and develops practical implications to realize the potential of the green economy in emerging market economies in the period until 2025.

Section 2 details the specifics of the impact of the COVID-19 crisis on sustainable development and the green economy in emerging market economies. It contains the modelling of the impact of the COVID-19 crisis on sustainable development and the green economy in emerging market economies in 2020–1. It also evaluates the consequences of implementing the measures of the fight against the pandemic and crisis in emerging market economies in 2020 for the green economy and sustainable development and conducts a case study of the impact of the COVID-19 crisis on sustainable development and the green economy in emerging market economies by the example of Russia in 2020–1.

Section 3 is devoted to the determination of the potential harm of the COVID-19 crisis to sustainable development and the green economy, as well as prospects of mitigating it – which is a new challenge for state management. The section presents the modelling of sustainable development and the green economy in 2020 – the harm of the crisis versus the harm of the anti-crisis measures. It develops economic policy implications to mitigate the harm of the COVID-19 crisis to sustainable development and the green economy based on a flexible combination of standard and alternative measures. It also performs a case study of using the alternative measures of the COVID-19 crisis management on the example of Russia in 2020–1.

In Section 4 (last by order, not importance), scenarios of sustainable development of emerging market economies amid the COVID-19 crisis and the prospects of anti-crisis management of the green economy are considered. It compares the impact of the COVID-19 pandemic on economic and green growth in emerging market economies in 2020, performs a scenario analysis of sustainable development of emerging market economies amid the COVID-19 crisis, and determines the prospects and develops recommendations in the sphere of anti-crisis management of the green economy for the COVID-19 crisis management in emerging market economies.

The Conclusion of the Element sums up the conducted scientific and practical research and presents a view of the future of emerging market economies in sustainable development based on the green economy amid the COVID-19 crisis.

## 1 The COVID-19 Crisis As a Barrier to the Formation of the Green Economy and Sustainable Development in Emerging Market Economies

### 1.1 Introduction

Formation of the green economy is one of the main directions of sustainable development of modern economic systems, together with the reduction of inequalities (SDG5 and SDG10), growth of quality of life (SDG1, SDG2, SDG3, and SDG4), economic progress (SDG8 and SDG9), and development of institutions (SDG16 and SDG17). A serious barrier on the path of the practical implementation of this direction, which is connected to the transition to the green economy, is the current narrow scientific view of this direction, which is limited by its target results that are adopted in SDG6, SDG7, SDG11, SDG12, SDG13, SDG14, and SDG15 (green SDGs).

A unilateral view of the green vector of sustainable development is presented in the works of Asongu and Odhiambo (2021), Dawid et al. (2021), Felício et al. (2021), Liu and Dong (2021), Ullah et al. (2021), Wang et al. (2021), and Ying et al. (2021). In these publications, the focus – when defining the notion of the green economy – is on a favourable environment and the low ecological costs of economic growth. A drawback of the existing unilateral view of the green economy is the uncertainty as to how environmental protection should be ensured, the obscurity of most of the prospective green economic initiatives, and, as a result, the inaccessibility of the levers of managing the process of establishment and development of the green economy (Bina, 2013).

The problem is as follows: this drawback is one of the most important reasons for the slow rate of green economy formation, especially in emerging market economies, where the social orientation and readiness for the transition to the green economy are insufficiently high (unlike advanced market economies) for this transition to take place naturally; thus there is an especial need for state regulation (unavailable or limited due to insufficient scientific support).

This problem is especially urgent because emerging market economies risk not only failing in the formation of the green economy in their territory but also threatening the global perspective of the achievement of the green SDGs by 2030, undermining the results of advanced market economies (Goyal & Sergi, 2015; Popkova & Sergi, 2020a). That's why there's a need for well-balanced results and substantial progress in the formation of the green economy in developing countries (Inshakov et al., 2019; Loiseau et al., 2016; Ponte, 2008; Popkova et al., 2019).

To overcome the described drawback, a systemic view of the green economy is offered; it covers ecological results and economic sources of achieving these results. The author's definition of the green economy is offered: a special type of economic system which features the active use of economic levers – green initiatives in the economy – to implement the green SDGs.

The value of the new definition is as follows. It significantly changes the perception of the green economy – for the first time, the environment ceases to be a resource for the economy – and of the aggravation of the environment's state – a consequence of economic development (ecological costs of economic growth). Instead of this, the economy becomes a resource (to be precise, a tool) of environment protection which in the most precise and correct way reflects the approach that envisages the implementation of the green SDGs. The discussion regarding the minimization of the economy's negative influence on the environment is a dead end for the implementation of the green SDGs; to find a way out of this dead end, it is necessary to search for the economy's potential to support, protect, and improve the environment's state. This is a completely new field for scientific research that requires elaboration.

Based on the domination of this unilateral scientific view of the green economy, the following hypothesis ($H_0$) is tested here: economic efficiency of the green SDGs was high even before the COVID-19 crisis (in 2019), but it grew further under the influence of the crisis (in 2020). This means that the economy's contribution to the improvement of the environment's state is very small – that is, the potential of the green economy's development has not been fully fulfilled. More active use of economic levers (fulfilment of the potential of the green economy's development) will allow for a substantial improvement of the environment's state by 2025 (the end of the second five-year period of the implementation of the SDGs).

This section intends to demonstrate that the high economic efficiency of the green SDGs is not a goal but something to avoid (not through the reduction of the results of the green SDGs but through the increase of the economy's contribution to their implementation). Green initiatives in the economy are not something to save economically (these are not expenditures to be reduced) but something to increase. The environment cannot protect itself, though, in reality, small-scale and underdeveloped green initiatives in the economy are based on such expectations. The economy should contribute to the protection of the environment, and this should become its priority.

The section studies the experience of the formation of the green economy and sustainable development in emerging market economies under the influence of the COVID-19 crisis, substantiating the fact that the green economy's potential in stimulating the implementation of the green SDGs has not been yet fulfilled, and developing recommendations for the fullest fulfilment of this potential of the green economy in emerging market economies in the period until 2025.

The uniqueness of this section consists in the complex (by the example of a large and representative sample), not fragmentary (by the example of one or several countries) study of the experience of formation of the green economy and sustainable development in emerging market economies, and in consideration of an especial context that formed in 2020 due to the COVID-19 crisis. The novelty and originality of this research are due to consideration not only of ecological results but also of their economic sources, which allows determining the following:

- influence of the COVID-19 crisis on the ecological results and the economic sources of their achievement, allowing for a comprehensive description of the green economy's development
- dependence of the ecological results on the economic sources
- economic efficiency of the green SDGs before and after the COVID-19 crisis, as well as the perspective of increasing it based on the utmost fulfilment of the potential of the green economy's development.

The practical implications of this section are due to its reflection of the case experience (successful examples) of implementing green initiatives in the Russian economy in 2020 amid the COVID-19 crisis. The set goal underscores the logic and structure of this research. This Introduction is followed by a literature review and a description of the methodology. The results include the following:

- study of the influence of the COVID-19 crisis on the green economy in emerging market economies
- consideration of the case experience (successful examples) of implementing green initiatives in the Russian economy in 2020 amid the COVID-19 crisis
- factor analysis of the influence of economic levers on the implementation of the green SDGs in emerging market economies
- development of practical implications to fulfil the potential of the green economy in emerging market economies in the period until 2025.

The Conclusion sums up the research.

## 1.2 Literature Review

Certain aspects of the influence of the COVID-19 crisis on the formation of the green economy and sustainable development are studied in the works of Adnan and Nordin (2021), Ali Shah et al. (2021), Bastida (2020), Brady (2019), Iyengar et al. (2021), Kaklauskas et al. (2021), Lahcen et al. (2020), Liu et al. (2021), Mayen Huerta and Cafagna (2021), Naeem et al. (2021a), Naeem et al. (2021b), Pan et al. (2021), and Spano et al. (2021).

Arif et al. (2021) study COVID-19 and determine the time and frequency connectedness between green and conventional financial markets. Mohideen et al. (2021) see the necessity of more active promotion of green energy solutions due to the COVID-19 pandemic. Fasan et al. (2021) conduct an empirical analysis and prove that a decrease in supply chain management of green materials became a consequence of COVID-19.

Berdejo-Espinola et al. (2021) study the use of urban green space during a time of stress and conduct a case study during the COVID-19 pandemic in Brisbane, Australia. Taghizadeh-Hesary et al. (2021) analyse the characteristics of green bond markets to facilitate green finance in the post–COVID-19 world. Ho et al. (2021) note the green marketing orientations towards sustainability in the hospitality industry during the COVID-19 pandemic.

Cai et al. (2021) offer green bed and breakfast (B&B) promotion strategies for tourist loyalty and perform a survey of the restart of Chinese national holiday travel after COVID-19. Ali Shah et al. (2021) deem it necessary to prioritize waste-to-energy technologies based on the energy trilemma and demonstrate the implications for post–COVID-19 green economic recovery in Pakistan. Mell and Whitten (2021) note the smaller access to nature in a post–COVID-19 world and consider the opportunities for green infrastructure financing, distribution, and equitability in urban planning.

The experience of the formation of the green economy and sustainable development in emerging market economies is given in the following works: Abid et al. (2021), Belmonte-Ureña et al. (2021), Bhopal et al. (2021), Dmuchowski et al. (2021), Howson (2021), and Mell and Whitten (2021).

Ali et al. (2021) prove that green economy implementation in Ghana is a road map for a sustainable development drive. Ullah et al. (2021) demonstrate a connection between information technology (IT) capability and green intellectual capital on sustainable businesses based on evidence from emerging economies. Felício et al. (2021) note the green shipping effect on sustainable economy and environmental performance.

Chairani (2021) thinks that disclosure of enterprise risk management in the countries of the Association of Southeast Asian Nations (ASEAN) 5 contributes to the sustainable development of the green economy. Odugbesan et al. (2021) point out that financial regulations matter for a sustainable green economy (based on the analysis of empirical evidence from Turkey). Mikhno et al. (2021) prove the important role of the green economy in sustainable development and resource efficiency.

Prakash and Sethi (2021) show that green bonds stimulate the sustainable transition in Asian economies (by the example of India). Liu et al. (2020) demonstrate that 'green food' certification could achieve both sustainable practices and economic benefits in a transitional economy (through the example of kiwi fruit growers in Henan Province, China).

Zhao et al. (2020) point out the impact of pollution regulation and technological investment on sustainable development of green economy in eastern China (through an empirical analysis that uses a panel data approach). Sharma (2020) proves that green management and a circular economy are very important for sustainable development. Kalikov et al. (2020) think that a green economy is a paradigm of sustainable development in the Republic of Kazakhstan.

The literature review allows stating that the level of the topic's elaboration is high; however, two research gaps exist. The first research gap is the fragmentary character of the study of the influence of the COVID-19 crisis on the formation of the green economy and sustainable development, which does not allow for the full picture of this influence. The second research gap is consideration of the experience of formation of the green economy and sustainable development only through the example of certain emerging market economies. This hinders the formation of the systemic understanding of the essence and specifics of the formation of the green economy and sustainable development in emerging market economies.

A serious drawback of the existing literature is that the connection between economy and environment is shown and studied only from one side. The environment is set at a lower level of the hierarchy, while the economy is set at a higher level. This completely contradicts the concept of sustainable development, which proclaims the equality of the economic, social, and ecological spheres of the economy.

The concept of sustainable development also envisages the bilateral relations of each sphere – at the intersection of the economic and ecological spheres, these bilateral relations mean, firstly, that the environment must help the development of the economy (immediate connection) and, secondly, that the economy must help the improvement of the environment's state (feedback). The immediate connection has been studied in detail and emphasized in existing work while feedback has been studied very poorly. This hinders building the green economy according to the concept of sustainable development.

To fill the existing gaps and overcome the drawback of the existing literature, this research does the following:

- studies the influence of the COVID-19 crisis on the formation of the green economy and sustainable development in emerging market economies based on continuous data on the whole complex of the green economy's manifestations with the comparison of the level of the green economy's development in 2019 (before the crisis) and in 2020 (after the crisis)
- considers a representative sample of emerging market economies, which allows applying the obtained results and conclusions to all countries of the same category
- covers a poorly studied sphere of the green economy: the contribution of green initiatives in the economy to the improvement of the environment's state.

## 1.3 Materials and Method

According to the set goal and formulated tasks, this research is conducted in five consecutive stages; the corresponding methods are applied at each stage. At stage 1, the influence of the COVID-19 crisis on the green economy in emerging market economies is studied. For this, trend analysis is applied to determine the change (in 2020 as compared to 2019) of the indicators from the materials of the Global Green Growth Institute (2021a, 2021b), which are divided into three blocks:

- Block 1 (results in the sphere of environment protection): efficient and sustainable resource use, which includes efficient and sustainable energy, efficient and sustainable water use, sustainable land use, and material use efficiency (Table 1)
- Block 2 (results in the sphere of environment protection): natural capital protection, which includes environmental quality, greenhouse gas (GHG) emissions reductions, biodiversity and ecosystem protection, and cultural and social value (Table 2)
- Block 3 (green initiatives in the economy – sources of the results): green economic opportunities, which include green investment, trade, employment, and innovation (Table 3).

To have a representative sample, nine emerging market economies from diverse geographical regions of the world (Africa, America, Asia, Europe, and Oceania) with different levels of green economic development are considered.

**Table 1** Efficient and sustainable resource use in emerging market economies in 2019–20, positions 1–100

| | | Efficient and sustainable energy use ($y_1$) | | Efficient and sustainable water use ($y_2$) | | Sustainable land use ($y_3$) | | Material use efficiency ($y_4$) | |
|---|---|---|---|---|---|---|---|---|---|
| | | 2019 | 2020 | 2019 | 2020 | 2019 | 2020 | 2019 | 2020 |
| Africa | Sao Tome and Principe | 77.34 | 74.24 | - | 51.76 | 76.10 | 99.94 | 90.16 | 90.17 |
| | Angola | 89.27 | 90.92 | 70.74 | 78.71 | 5.17 | 50.48 | 94.22 | 94.23 |
| | Nigeria | 83.66 | 79.84 | 51.73 | 56.08 | 4.63 | 50.65 | 94.09 | 94.11 |
| America | Guatemala | 87.94 | 86.68 | 52.89 | 53.72 | 17.72 | 50.68 | 91.90 | 91.90 |
| | Honduras | 81.99 | 81.48 | 51.64 | 52.62 | 21.27 | 53.01 | 89.97 | 89.98 |
| | Panama | 67.11 | 68.07 | 57.77 | 59.10 | 8.42 | 52.90 | 95.51 | 95.50 |
| Asia | Cambodia | 83.34 | 82.21 | 51.13 | 51.48 | 8.49 | 51.05 | 80.89 | 80.90 |
| | Philippines | 69.71 | 65.57 | 50.93 | 47.69 | 14.10 | 56.63 | 93.27 | 93.28 |
| | Bangladesh | 76.67 | 74.01 | 51.04 | 51.45 | 12.47 | 48.85 | 88.00 | 87.99 |
| Europe | Slovenia | 58.19 | 57.22 | 56.16 | 58.34 | 47.87 | 76.97 | 85.02 | 85.01 |
| | Belarus | 37.87 | 36.96 | 56.35 | 56.35 | - | - | 89.55 | 89.54 |
| | Russia | 27.62 | 26.55 | 52.48 | 53.85 | 15.75 | 51.02 | 89.51 | 89.50 |
| Oceania | Samoa | 68.89 | 64.71 | - | - | 75.52 | 100.00 | 92.19 | 92.19 |
| | Papua New Guinea | 70.85 | 83.03 | 55.61 | - | 37.18 | 55.63 | 78.82 | 78.81 |
| | Fiji | 67.22 | 64.58 | 56.26 | 57.21 | 39.26 | 63.40 | 93.66 | 93.66 |

**Source:** Compiled by the author based on Global Green Growth Institute (2021a, 2021b)

**Table 2** Natural capital protection in emerging market economies in 2019–20, position 1–100

| | | Environmental quality | | Greenhouse gas emissions reductions | | Biodiversity and ecosystem protection | | Cultural and social value | |
|---|---|---|---|---|---|---|---|---|---|
| | | 2019 | 2020 ($y_5$) | 2019 | 2020 ($y_6$) | 2019 | 2020 ($y_7$) | 2019 | 2020 ($y_8$) |
| Africa | Sao Tome and Principe | 91.32 | 85.79 | 96.01 | 96.66 | 81.03 | 71.93 | 50.89 | 44.77 |
| | Angola | 60.83 | 63.43 | 75.40 | 73.49 | 59.79 | 47.71 | 44.51 | 44.35 |
| | Nigeria | 34.13 | 49.17 | 90.50 | 89.58 | 58.20 | 44.24 | 58.73 | 55.04 |
| America | Guatemala | 83.96 | 83.56 | 89.38 | 87.40 | 76.53 | 53.90 | 50.00 | 49.15 |
| | Honduras | 85.27 | 86.07 | 88.95 | 81.20 | 82.28 | 61.56 | 59.10 | 49.66 |
| | Panama | 88.01 | 88.40 | 85.78 | 76.79 | 77.38 | 58.04 | 53.36 | 52.65 |
| Asia | Cambodia | 91.47 | 89.33 | 81.38 | 78.08 | 72.19 | 55.15 | 89.17 | 88.53 |
| | Philippines | 90.32 | 90.79 | 91.33 | 91.83 | 76.81 | 65.05 | 39.26 | 56.91 |
| | Bangladesh | 70.06 | 73.59 | 92.36 | 92.83 | 56.88 | 32.84 | 36.72 | 36.00 |
| Europe | Slovenia | 87.51 | 87.24 | 69.49 | 80.32 | 77.51 | 83.69 | 76.84 | 76.54 |
| | Belarus | 87.01 | 86.17 | 57.63 | 63.62 | 55.67 | 62.47 | 82.26 | 82.38 |
| | Russia | 88.68 | 87.72 | 42.82 | 42.23 | 56.99 | 49.05 | 54.34 | 53.49 |
| Oceania | Samoa | 95.09 | 94.55 | 87.61 | 80.20 | 61.80 | 45.86 | 52.23 | 49.51 |
| | Papua New Guinea | 82.02 | 81.34 | 89.16 | 83.61 | 60.89 | 49.23 | 28.31 | 28.41 |
| | Fiji | 91.84 | 91.22 | 86.39 | 81.05 | 62.66 | 52.22 | 50.96 | 51.32 |

**Source:** Compiled by the author based on Global Green Growth Institute (2021a, 2021b)

**Table 3** Green economic opportunities in emerging market economies in 2019–20, position 1–100

| | | Green investment | | Green trade | | Green employment | | Green innovation | |
|---|---|---|---|---|---|---|---|---|---|
| | | 2019 | 2020 ($x_1$) | 2019 | 2020 ($x_2$) | 2019 | 2020 ($x_3$) | 2019 | 2020 ($x_4$) |
| Africa | Sao Tome and Principe | - | - | 1.44 | 10.22 | - | - | - | - |
| | Angola | - | 12.47 | 36.97 | 2.03 | - | 15.18 | - | - |
| | Nigeria | 57.13 | 55.79 | 1.07 | 1.31 | 1.00 | 1.00 | - | - |
| America | Guatemala | 59.04 | 57.85 | 15.79 | 6.64 | - | 1.01 | 14.03 | 7.59 |
| | Honduras | 80.61 | 78.36 | 3.20 | 4.87 | - | - | 14.03 | 12.37 |
| | Panama | 88.87 | 85.82 | 10.45 | 8.35 | 15.56 | 10.84 | 1.00 | 1.00 |
| Asia | Cambodia | 69.83 | 67.55 | 2.68 | 2.86 | 1.00 | 1.06 | - | - |
| | Philippines | 94.61 | 80.20 | 41.05 | 17.16 | 51.96 | 38.75 | 27.05 | 16.42 |
| | Bangladesh | 91.12 | 81.97 | 2.46 | 2.30 | - | 13.79 | - | - |
| Europe | Slovenia | 66.46 | 69.55 | 44.28 | 35.93 | 73.79 | 62.56 | 14.03 | 44.44 |
| | Belarus | 82.13 | 74.07 | 18.28 | 14.2 | 15.56 | 54.90 | 1.00 | 1.00 |
| | Russia | 66.75 | 65.33 | 11.18 | 8.29 | 95.63 | 87.53 | 27.05 | 40.23 |
| Oceania | Samoa | - | - | 2.46 | 18.60 | - | - | - | - |
| | Papua New Guinea | - | - | - | - | - | - | - | - |
| | Fiji | 66.76 | - | 94.73 | 4.39 | 1.00 | 85.34 | - | - |

**Source:** Compiled by the author based on Global Green Growth Institute (2021a, 2021b)

The economic efficiency of the green SDGs is calculated according to the following formula:

$$GE_{EconEffic} = GE_{Res}/GE_{Souces}, \qquad (1)$$

where $GE_{EconEffic}$ – economic efficiency of the green SDGs;
$GE_{Res}$ – results in the sphere of the implementation of the green SDGs; and
$GE_{Sources}$ – green initiatives in the economy (Block 3: sources of the results).

According to formula (1), the economic efficiency of the green SDGs is the ratio of the results in the sphere of implementing the green SDGs to green initiatives in the economy (Block 3: sources of the results).

The results in the sphere of implementing the green SDGs are the arithmetic mean of Blocks 1 and 2, which is calculated according to the following formula:

$$GE_{Results} = (GE_{Res1} + GE_{Res2})/2, \qquad (2)$$

where $GE_{Res1}$ – efficient and sustainable resource use (Block 1: results in the sphere of environment protection); and
$GE_{Res2}$ – natural capital protection (Block 2: results in the sphere of environment protection).

Values for each of the three blocks are calculated as the sum of all indicators of the block, according to the following formulas:

$$GE_{Sources} = x_1 + x_2 + x_3 + x_4, \qquad (3)$$

$$GE_{Res1} = y_1 + y_2 + y_3 + y_4, \text{ and} \qquad (4)$$

$$GE_{Res2} = y_5 + y_6 + y_7 + y_8. \qquad (5)$$

The evaluation's results are treated in the following way:
$GE_{EconEffic} \leq 0.5$: very low economic efficiency of the green SDGs;
$0.5 < GE_{EconEffic} < 1$: low economic efficiency of the green SDGs;
$GE_{EconEffic} = 1$: zero economic efficiencies of the green SDGs;
$1 < GE_{EconEffic} \leq 1.5$: medium economic efficiency of the green SDGs;
$1.5 < GE_{EconEffic} < 2$: high economic efficiency of the green SDGs; and
$GE_{EconEffic} \geq 2$: very high economic efficiency of the green SDGs.

The scientific and economic sense of the offered hypothesis is as follows: (both conditions must be observed simultaneously – i.e., they are mutually reinforcing, not mutually exclusive):

- Condition 1 of hypothesis $H_0$: even before the COVID-19 crisis – that is, in 2019 – economic efficiency of the green SDGs was very high ($GE_{EconEffic2019} \geq 2$).

- Condition 2 of hypothesis $H_0$: under the influence of the COVID-19 crisis – that is, in 2020 – economic efficiency of the green SDGs further increased ($GE_{EconEffic2020} > GE_{EconEffic2019}$).

At stage 2, successful examples of implementing green initiatives in the Russian economy in 2020 – amid the COVID-19 crisis – are analysed with the help of the case study. At stage 3, the factor analysis is performed of the influence of economic levers on the implementation of the green SDGs in emerging market economies. For this regression analysis is used to compile the equation of multiple linear regression of the following form (for each $y_1 - y_8$):

$$y = a + b_1 * x_1 + b_2 * x_2 + b_3 * x_3 + b_4 * x_4, \tag{6}$$

At stage 4, the practical implications of fulfilling the potential of the green economy in emerging market economies in the period until 2025 are developed. For this the simplex method is used to determine the optimal combination of factor variables ($x_1 - x_4$) at which the largest growth of the resulting variables ($y_1 - y_8$) is ensured. The economic efficiency of the green SDGs is also assessed, which has to reduce due to the optimization by 2025.

## 1.4 Results

### *1.4.1 The Influence of the COVID-19 Crisis on the Green Economy in Emerging Market Economies*

To determine the character (positive or negative) and scale (in the quantitative measuring) of the influence of the COVID-19 crisis on the green economy in emerging market economies, the method of trend analysis is used to study the dynamics of the change of the indicators from Tables 1–3 in 2020 as compared to 2019 (Figure 1).

As shown in Figure 1, efficient and sustainable energy reduces in 2020 as compared to 2019 by 1.11% under the influence of the COVID-19 crisis; efficient and sustainable water use reduced by 4.89%. Sustainable land use grew by 124.30%, and material use efficiency remained unchanged. On the whole, for Block 1, efficient and sustainable resource use grew by 29.58%, which shows a significant improvement in the sphere of environment protection under the influence of the COVID-19 crisis.

Environmental quality grew by 0.88%, GHG emissions reductions slowed down by 2.07%, biodiversity and ecosystem protection reduced by 18.07%, and cultural and social value reduced by 0.96%. On the whole, for Block 2, natural capital protection was reduced by 5.05%, which shows a contradictory influence of the COVID-19 crisis on the results in the sphere of environment protection.

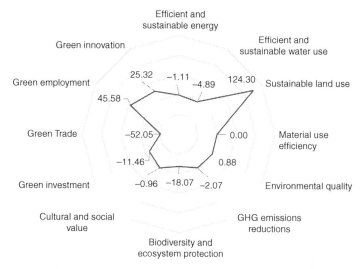

**Figure 1** Trend analysis of the green economy in emerging market economies in 2020 as compared to 2019 (growth), %. *Source*: Author

Green investment reduced by 11.46% and green trade reduced by 52.0%. However, green employment grew by 45.58%, and green innovation grew by 25.32%. On the whole, for Block 3, green economic opportunities grew by 1.85%, though green initiatives in the economy (the source of the results) were subject to the contradictory influence of the COVID-19 crisis.

Let us perform calculations for 2019 and evaluate the economic efficiency of the green SDGs. For this, we determine the values for each block (on average for the whole sample):

$$\begin{aligned}
GE_{Sources2019} &= 69.84 + 51.05 + 25.60 + 89.78 = 236.28; \\
GE_{Res12019} &= 81.83 + 81.61 + 67.77 + 55.11 = 286.33; \\
GE_{Res22019} &= 54.89 + 19.07 + 17.03 + 6.55 = 97.54.
\end{aligned}$$

Then we calculate the results in the sphere of implementing the green SDGs:

$$GE_{Results2019} = (GE_{Res12019} + GE_{Res22019})/2 = (236.28 + 286.33)/2 = 261.31.$$

Let us calculate the economic efficiency of the green SDGs:

$$GE_{EconEffic2019} = GE_{Res2019}/GE_{Sources2019} = 261.31/97.54 = 2.68.$$

Since the obtained value $GE_{EconEffic2019} \geq 2$, the economic efficiency of the green SDGs was very high in 2019 (condition 1 of hypothesis $H_0$ is observed).

Let us perform similar calculations for 2020. Let us evaluate the economic efficiency of the green SDGs. For this we determine the values for each block (on average for the whole sample):

$$
\begin{aligned}
GE_{Sources2020} &= 69.07 + 48.56 + 57.41 + 89.78 = 264.83; \\
GE_{Res12020} &= 82.56 + 79.93 + 55.53 + 54.58 = 272.59; \\
GE_{Res22020} &= 48.60 + 9.14 + 24.80 + 8.20 = 903.74.
\end{aligned}
$$

Let us calculate the results in the sphere of implementing the green SDGs:

$$
GE_{Results2020} = (GE_{Res12020} + GE_{Res22020})/2 = (264.83 + 272.59)/2 = 268.71.
$$

Let us determine the economic efficiency of the green SDGs:

$$
GE_{EconEffic2020} = GE_{Res2020}/GE_{Sources2020} = 268.71/90.74 = 2.96.
$$

Since the obtained value $GE_{EconEffic2020} \geq 2$, the economic efficiency of the green SDGs was very high in 2020. $GE_{EconEffic2020} > GE_{EconEffic2019}(2.96 > 2.68)$ (condition 2 of hypothesis $H_0$ is observed).

### 1.4.2 Case Experience (Successful Examples) of Implementing Green Initiatives in the Russian Economy in 2020 amid the COVID-19 Crisis

Let us consider successful examples of implementing green initiatives in the Russian economy in 2020 amid the COVID-19 crisis. According to Forbes (2021), in the ranking of the top thirty ecological companies of Russia in 2020, the first place belonged to Mars, which specializes in the food industry. In 2020, this company improved its results in the sphere of food stock recycling.

The second position belongs to the largest Russian bank – Sberbank – which increased the volume of green investment by eight times in 2020 (as compared to 2019), up to RUB 47 billion. It is expedient to also consider the successful experience of a retail company, the X5 Retail Group (ranked third), which expanded its corporate programme of recycling in 2020 and adopted a strategy according to which it will reduce GHG emissions by 10% and increase the share of recycled food products up to 40% until 2023.

Russia's case experience has shown that a lot of ecologically responsible companies continued implementing and even expanding their successful corporate green initiatives amid the COVID-19 crisis. At the same time, in emerging market economies, these companies are presented mainly by transnational corporations, due to which wide groups of business structures are not involved in the green economy.

### 1.4.3 Factor Analysis of the Influence of Economic Levers on Implementing the Green Sustainable Development Goals in Emerging Market Economies

To determine the contribution of green initiatives in the economy to the formation of results in the sphere of the green SDGs implementation, the data from Tables 1–3 are used to conduct factor analysis (with the help of regression analysis based on the data for 2020) – its results are shown in Table 4.

The obtained results of the regression analysis demonstrate that economic levers (green initiatives in the economy) are not universal – they provide support for certain results on implementing the green SDGs but slow down the implementation of other green SDGs. Therefore, there's a need for large flexibility and care during the use of economic levers. A general vision of the perspectives of improving their use is not obvious, as there is not a single economic lever that would have a non-negative influence on all results on the implementation of the green SDGs (i.e., 'manual' optimization is unavailable). That is why it is expedient to formulate and solve the optimization task with the use of automatization.

### 1.4.4 Practical Implications for Fulfilling the Potential of the Green Economy in Emerging Market Economies in the Period until 2025

To determine the potential of the green economy in emerging market economies in the period until 2025, the following task of poly-parametric non-linear optimization has been formulated:

- goal: maximization of the values of the resulting variables $y_1 - y_8$
- changed factor variables: $x_1 - x_4$
- limitation: values of the factor variables ($x_1 - x_4$) after the optimization must not be lower than their values in 2020.

The task is solved in Microsoft Excel with the help of the 'Solution Search' function. The contradictory influence of economic levers on the results in the sphere of implementing the green SDGs does not allow finding the only solution to the formulate optimization task. Instead of this, its solution (in this case) is a set of Pareto efficiencies. To choose the most preferable one, the priority is set additionally (desirable but not mandatory condition): the values of the resulting variables ($y_1 - y_8$) after optimization must not be lower than their values in 2020. The selected most preferable Pareto efficiency is shown in Figure 2.

The obtained and presented results (Figure 2) (Pareto optimality) allow recommending the following practical implications for fulfilling the potential of the green economy in emerging market economies in the period until 2025:

**Table 4** Regression statistics of the influence of economic levers on implementing the green SDGs in emerging market economies in 2020

| Regression statistics | $y_1$ | $y_2$ | $y_3$ | $y_4$ | $y_5$ | $y_6$ | $y_7$ | $y_8$ |
|---|---|---|---|---|---|---|---|---|
| Constant a | 86.06 | 34.51 | 76.48 | 88.12 | 76.64 | 83.50 | 47.67 | 35.47 |
| Coefficient $b_1$ (at $x_1$) | −0.09 | 0.27 | −0.47 | 0.02 | −0.01 | −0.01 | 0.00 | 0.22 |
| Coefficient $b_2$ (at $x_2$) | −0.38 | −0.44 | 0.81 | 0.08 | 0.59 | 0.54 | 0.89 | 0.91 |
| Coefficient $b_3$ (at $x_3$) | −0.40 | 0.25 | −0.38 | 0.05 | 0.09 | −0.20 | −0.03 | 0.15 |
| Coefficient $b_4$ (at $x_4$) | 0.08 | −0.13 | 0.72 | −0.16 | −0.14 | −0.35 | 0.09 | −0.46 |

**Source:** Author

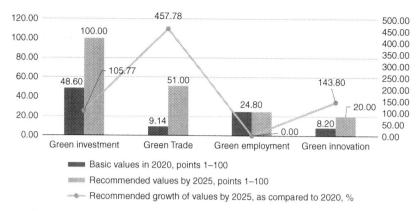

**Figure 2** Pareto efficiency for fulfilling the green economy's potential in emerging market economies in the period until 2025. *Source:* Author

- increase of green investment from 48.60 points to the maximum 100 points – that is, by 105.77%
- increase of green trade from 9.14 points to 51 points – that is, by 457.78%
- increase of green innovation from 8.20 points to 20 points – that is, by 143.80%.

Green employment remains unchanged (at the 2020 level) until 2025 (24.80 points). In this case:

$$GE_{Sources2025} = 100 + 51 + 24.80 + 20 = 195.80.$$

In Block 3 (green initiatives in economy – source of the results), green economic opportunities in 2025 (195.80) will become much higher than in 2020, when it was 90.74. This means that optimization will allow for larger use of economic levers. The consequences of fulfilling this potential of the green economy in emerging market economies in the period until 2025 are shown in Figure 3.

As shown in Figure 3, the consequences of fulfilling the green economy's potential in emerging market economies in the period until 2025 include the following:

- increase of sustainable land use from 57.41 points to 75.53 points – that is, by 31.55%
- increase of material use efficiency from 89.78 points to 92.39 points – that is, by 2.91%.

Efficient and sustainable energy will decrease by 28.37% and efficient and sustainable water use will decrease by 12.78%. In this case:

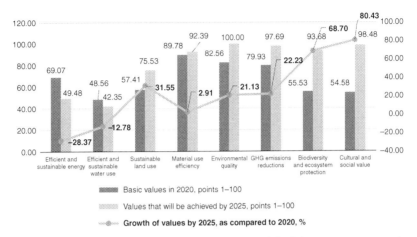

Figure 3 The consequences of fulfilling the potential of the green economy in
emerging market economies in the period until 2025. *Source*: Author

$$GE_{Res12025} = 49.48 + 42.35 + 75.53 + 92.39 = 259.75.$$

In Block 1 (results in the sphere of environment protection), efficient and
sustainable resource use (259.75) will become lower in 2025 than in 2020,
when it equalled 264.83. The consequences of fulfilling the potential of the
green economy in emerging market economies in the period until 2025 also
include the following:

- growth of environmental quality from 82.56 points to 100 points – that is, by
  27.50%
- increase of the level of GHG emissions reductions from 79.93 points to 97.69
  points – that is, by 22.23%
- growth of biodiversity and ecosystem protection from 55.53 points to 93.68
  points – that is, by 68.70%
- increase of cultural and social value from 54.58 points to 98.48 points – that
  is, by 80.43%.

In this case:

$$GE_{Res22025} = 100 + 97.69 + 93.68 + 98.48 = 389.85.$$

In Block 2 (results in the sphere of environment protection), natural capital
protection in 2025 (389.85) will grow compared to 2020, when the value was
272.59. The aggregate results in the sphere of implementing the green SDGs in
2025 will be as follows:

$$GE_{Results2025} = (GE_{Res12025} + GE_{Res22025})/2 = (259.75 + 389.85)/2 = 324.80.$$

The aggregate results in the sphere of implementing the green SDGs in 2025 (324.80) will be much higher than in 2020 (268.71). Economic efficiency of the green SDGs in 2025 will equal:

$$GE_{EconEffic2020} = GE_{Res2020}/GE_{Sources2020} = 324.80/195.80 = 1.66.$$

Since the obtained value $1.5 < GE_{EconEffic} < 2$, there will be high economic efficiency of the green SDGs in 2025, which, however, will be below its 2020 level (2.96).

## 1.5 Conclusion

Thus, as a result of the conducted research, it has been determined that the COVID-19 crisis has become a barrier to the formation of the green economy and sustainable development in emerging market economies. Though under the influence of the COVID-19 crisis, natural capital protection reduced by 5.05%, a more significant barrier (as compared to the crisis) to the formation of the green economy and sustainable development in emerging market economies is very limited green initiatives in the economy.

From the results, the influence of the COVID-19 crisis on the formation of the green economy and sustainable development in emerging market economies could be considered positive since efficient and sustainable resource use grew by 29.58% as compared to 2019. However, from the positions of the source of the results, the COVID-19 crisis had a negative influence – green investment decreased by 11.46% in 2020 (as compared to 2019) and green trade decreased by 52.0%.

The influence of the COVID-19 crisis on the formation of the green economy and sustainable development in emerging market economies is characterized most precisely and correctly by the economic efficiency of the green SDGs, which in 2020 (2.96) grew by 10.45% as compared to 2019 (2.68). That is, the COVID-19 crisis further limited the use of economic levers of environmental protection. However, as the case of Russia has shown, many ecologically responsible companies continued implementing and even expanded their successful corporate green initiatives amid the COVID-19 crisis.

To reduce the negative influence of the COVID-19 crisis in the period until 2025, the practical implications for fulfilling the potential of the green economy in emerging market economies are offered:

- increase of green investment by 105.77%
- increase of green trade by 457.78%
- increase of green innovation by 143.80%.

The advantages of fulfilling the potential of the green economy in emerging market economies in the period until 2025 include the following:

- increase of sustainable land use by 31.55%
- increase of material use efficiency by 2.91%
- growth of environmental quality by 27.50%
- increase of the scale of GHG emissions reductions by 22.23%
- growth of biodiversity and ecosystem protection by 68.70%
- increase of cultural and social value by 80.43%.

Due to the practical implementation of the offered recommendations, the aggregate results in the sphere of implementing the green SDGs in 2025 (324.80) will be much higher than in 2020 (268.71). The economic efficiency of the green SDGs in 2025 will equal 1.66, which is much lower than in 2020 (2.96). The contribution of green initiatives in the economy to environment protection will grow by 43.92%. This will allow for the fullest and most effective use of economic levers of environment protection. The contribution of this research to literature consists in developing a new scientific and meth-odological approach to green economy management through which economic levers of environment protection are used to the full extent and green initiatives in the economy perform the key role in implementing the green SDGs.

## 2 Specific Nature of the Impact of the COVID-19 Crisis on Sustainable Development and the Green Economy in Emerging Market Economies

### 2.1 Introduction

The COVID-19 crisis is unique. All previous crises had – directly or indirectly – an economic basis (imbalance of demand and offer). A vivid example is the Great Recession of 2008, which was caused by the oversaturation of financial markets (crisis of overproduction). In the conditions of the Great Recession, the efficiency of the market mechanism was temporarily reduced and later success-fully overcome by state regulation, which has to stimulate economic growth. The influence of a crisis on the economy is unambiguously negative and is associated with a sharp increase in unemployment, a decrease in business activities, investors' losses, and a temporary reduction of corporate social responsibility and growth of environmental costs of the further (post-crisis) economic growth (Popkova & Sergi, 2020b).

  The contrast between the 2008 Great Recession and the COVID-19 crisis is very clear since the COVID-19 crisis was caused by non-economic reasons (healthcare issues) and its consequences are ambiguous. The efficiency of the market mechanism amid the COVID-19 crisis remained unchanged; the activities of most markets were manually limited or stopped due to the lockdown. State regulation has to overcome the viral threat (primarily), while the stimulation of economic growth must not be allowed to fall by the wayside. Total limitations of business activities and the requirement of self-isolation were implemented at the expense of economic growth in order to reduce COVID-19 cases.

Since there is no crisis of overproduction and demand is preserved, the unemployment rate does not grow; instead of firing employees, companies have transferred them to remote work. Business activities are being restored rapidly in the course of the cancellation of limitations and its reduction amid the lockdown is not that significant due to companies' transition to online work. Investors do not suffer gigantic losses. On the contrary, they move their attention to the growing markets of healthcare and increase their capital (Popkova & Sergi, 2020d). Corporate social responsibility grows because society's attention is focussed on it. Environmental costs also reduce due to increased public-private monitoring and corporate social responsibility.

All of these factors add to the great importance of studying the COVID-19 crisis from the position of sustainable development. Special attention should be paid to the experience of emerging market economies for the following reasons. Firstly, existing literature (Nundy et al., 2021; Popkova et al., 2020; Popkova & Sergi, 2021) shows that a green economy is associated with sustainable development. According to the experience of advanced market economies, the COVID-19 crisis slowed the rate of development of the green economy and the implementation of the SDG). However, this cannot be unambiguously applied to emerging market economies (Chen & Golley, 2014). Unlike advanced market economies, in which successful results in implementing the SDGs are equal, the results in emerging market economies are different. That is why the COVID-19 pandemic might have different influences on the green economy and sustainable development.

Secondly, also based on the experience of advanced market economies in the existing literature (Al Asbahi et al., 2020; Lazzini et al., 2021), a negative impact of the COVID-19 crisis on the green economy and sustainable development due to the outflow of investments towards healthcare and economic growth is acknowledged. However, as certain examples show, the lockdown made a positive contribution to the green economy and sustainable development. For example, energy consumption and carbon emissions (environment pollution) were reduced during the lockdown, especially in emerging market economies (Popkova & Sergi, 2020a).

The experience and the specifics of the impact of the COVID-19 crisis on sustainable development and the green economy in emerging market economies thus have been studied insufficiently. The resulting application of the measures of economic crisis management, without consideration of the consequences for the green economy and sustainable development, could cause serious, unexpected, and negative externalities that could have been avoided if better awareness and scientific substantiation of the used measures were practised (Biswas & Roy, 2015).

This research aims to determine the specific nature of the impact of the COVID-19 crisis on sustainable development and the green economy in emerging market economies. The uniqueness of this research resides in the differentiation of the green economy and sustainable development because of the specifics of emerging market economies (differences in achievement of the results for different SDGs). This allows separate consideration of the impact of the COVID-19 pandemic on the green economy and sustainable development, as well as determining and specifying the differences of the consequences for them.

The novelty of this research is that it is a deep and systemic study of the experience of emerging market economies in the influence of economic crisis management measures on the green economy and sustainable development. Refusal from the a priori acknowledgement of the negative impact allows determination of the possible positive impact. The originality of this research rests in reconsideration of the current measures of fighting the pandemic and crisis through the lens of the consequences for the green economy and sustainable development. This offers a well-balanced approach to the fight against the pandemic, which ensures, at the same time, economic crisis management (stimulation of economic growth) and support for the green economy and sustainable development.

This introduction is followed by the literature review, description of materials and methodology, and results, which secure the solution of the following research tasks:

- Model of the impact of the COVID-19 crisis on sustainable development and the green economy in emerging market economies in 2020–1
- Assessment of the consequences of implementing the measures of fighting the pandemic in emerging market economies in 2020 for the green economy and sustainable development
- Case study of the impact of the COVID-19 crisis on sustainable development and the green economy in an emerging market economy: Russia in 2020–1.

## 2.2 Literature Review

The impact of the COVID-19 crisis on sustainable development and the green economy has been thoroughly researched in numerous studies.

Veter et al. (2021) note the 'back to nature' tendency and describe the Norwegian sustained increase of recreational use of urban green space months after the COVID-1 outbreak. Arif et al. (2021) determine the time–frequency connection between COVID-1 and the green and conventional financial markets.

Naeem et al. (2021) report that COVID-19 influences the connection between green bonds and other financial markets. These scholars analysed the evidence from the time–frequency domain with portfolio implications. Ali Shah et al. (2021) indicate that energy trilemma-based prioritization of waste-to-energy technologies is necessary and describe the implications for post–COVID-19 green economic recovery in Pakistan.

Sun et al. (2021) describe the impact of the COVID-19 pandemic on green consumption behaviour in China, while Wang and Huang (2021) prove the significant consequences of COVID-19 for SDGs. Chen et al. (2021) outline the challenges of the COVID-19 control policies for sustainable development of business based on evidence from service industries, and Chae (2021) demonstrates the effects of the COVID-19 pandemic on sustainable consumption.

The COVID-19 crisis and the implementation of anti-crisis measures in emerging market economies has been investigated by Hassankhani et al. (2021), who draw a connection between smart city and crisis management and determining lessons learned from the COVID-19 pandemic. Kuzmynchuk et al. (2021) offer a paradigm for ensuring energy saving in crisis management conditions of sustainable environmental development.

Abo Murad et al. (2021) investigate crisis management strategies in the Jordanian hotel industry, while Wodak (2021) compares crisis communication and crisis management during the COVID-19 pandemic and Fasth et al. (2021) address crisis management as a practice in small- and medium-sized enterprises during the first period of COVID-19. Nam and Nam (2021) outline the strategic directions of pandemic crisis management based on a text analysis of the World Economic Forum's COVID-19 reports.

This literature review reveals a serious drawback in the existing literature, where the green economy is associated with sustainable development; in the conditions of the pandemic in emerging market economies, they should be differentiated due to the potential differences in the consequences of the crisis and anti-crisis measures on them.

There are two research gaps. The first research gap is the poor elaboration of the consequences of the COVID-19 crisis for sustainable development and the green economy in emerging market economies. This leads to the lack of an evidence base for proving or disproving the fact that the impact of the COVID-19 crisis on sustainable development and the green economy in emerging market economies is unambiguously negative, similar to advanced market economies.

The second research gap is the insufficient elaboration of the measures of economic crisis management from the positions of the consequences of their use for the green economy and sustainable development in emerging market economies. A 'blind' application of these measures could lead to unreasonably elevated environmental costs of economic growth in the post-crisis economy and incomplete implementation of the potential reduction of these costs. This research aims to fill these gaps through a deep study of the specific nature of the impact of the COVID-19 crisis on sustainable development and the green economy in emerging market economies.

## 2.3 Materials and Method

### 2.3.1 Research Hypotheses

The following hypotheses are offered and tested in this section:

Hypothesis $H_1$: The COVID-19 crisis has had different impacts on sustainable development and green economies in emerging market economies, both negatively and positively.

Hypothesis $H_2$: The current measures of fighting the pandemic in emerging market economies ensure only economic crisis management (stimulation of economic growth) while providing insufficient (incomplete implementation of the potential) support for the green economy and sustainable development.

### 2.3.2 Methodology and Empirical Data

To test hypothesis $H_1$, one of the most precise methods of econometrics – regression analysis – is used. The impact of the COVID-19 pandemic and crisis on sustainable development (SD) (the Sustainable Development Index (SDI) is calculated by the United Nations Development Programme (UNDP) (2021)) and the green economy (the Green Growth (GG) Index is calculated by the Global Green Growth Institute, 2021) in emerging market economies is determined. The factors of the COVID-19 pandemic and crisis are as follows:

- Number of COVID-19 cases per 1 million people (cs): calculated for the compatibility of data for countries with different populations based on the materials of the World Health Organization (2021) on the current number of cases and population of countries in 2021 of the International Monetary Fund (2021)

- The economic growth rate in 2020, % (as compared to 2019): based on the materials of the International Monetary Fund (2021)
- Self-isolation index, points 1–100 (si): based on the materials of the Institute of Scientific Communications (2021d).

The research model has the following form:

$$\begin{cases} GG = a_{gg} + b_{gg1} * cs + b_{gg2} * eg + b_{gg3} * si \\ SD = a_{sd} + b_{sd1} * cs + b_{sd2} * eg + b_{sd3} * si \end{cases} \qquad (7)$$

The logic of testing hypothesis $H_1$ is the determination of either simultaneously positive influence of the factors of the COVID-19 crisis on the green economy ($b_{gg1} > 0$ and/or $b_{gg2} > 0$ and/or $b_{gg3} > 0$) with the negative influence of these factors on sustainable development ($b_{sd1} < 0$ and/or $b_{sd2} < 0$ and/or $b_{sd3} < 0$), or simultaneously negative impact of the factors of the COVID-19 crisis on the green economy ($b_{gg1} < 0$ and/or $b_{gg2} < 0$ and/or $b_{gg3} < 0$) with the positive influence of these factors on sustainable development ($b_{sd1} > 0$ and/or $b_{sd2}.0$ and/or $b_{sd3}.0$). That is, the sign of the coefficients b in research model (7) should be different.

A representative sample has been formed for the research; it contains emerging market economies from different regions of the world with different rates of green growth and sustainable development (according to the Global Green Growth Institute, 2021).

The empirical data for the research are given in Table 5.

Hypothesis $H_2$ is tested with the help of correlation analysis as per Saaty's hierarchy procedure. Correlation analysis is used to determine the character of the connection (positive or negative) between the results from Table 5 (the Green Growth Index and the SDI) and the measures of the fight against the pandemic and crisis in emerging market economies in 2020 (Table 6).

Based on the correlation coefficients obtained, the weight coefficients are calculated; they reflect the systemic contribution of each measure to the green economy and sustainable development. Saaty's method is used to determine the aggregate contribution of all implemented measures to the green economy and sustainable development in emerging market economies in 2020. Hypothesis $H_2$ is considered proved if the contribution is small (less than 40 points).

To supplement quantitative research with a qualitative study and to perform a deep analysis of the impact of the COVID-19 crisis on sustainable development and the green economy in emerging market economies, a case study of Russia in 2020–1 is performed.

**Table 5** The factors of the COVID-19 pandemic and crisis and the statistics of sustainable development and the green economy in emerging market economies in 2020–1

| | | Results | | Factors of the COVID-19 pandemic and crisis | | | | |
| --- | --- | --- | --- | --- | --- | --- | --- | --- |
| Region | Country | Green Growth Index, score 1–100 | Sustainable Development Index, score 1–100 | Cases – cumulative total | Population, thousand people | Cases – cumulative total, per 1,000 people | Gross domestic product, constant prices, % change | Self-isolation index, points 1–100 |
| | | GG | SD | – | – | cs | eg | si |
| Africa | South Africa | 48.79 | 63.74 | 2,447,454 | 60,531 | 0.0404 | –6.960 | n/a |
| | Kenya | 38.36 | 60.60 | 203,213 | 49,801 | 0.0041 | –0.127 | n/a |
| America | Mexico | 61.64 | 69.13 | 2,848,252 | 128,972 | 0.0221 | –8.239 | 48 |
| | Brazil | 55.18 | 71.34 | 19,917,855 | 212,781 | 0.0936 | –4.059 | 44 |
| Asia | China | 58.33 | 72.06 | 120,837 | 1,408,095 | 0.0001 | 2.270 | n/a |
| | India | 43.54 | 60.07 | 31,695,958 | 1,391,986 | 0.0228 | –7.965 | 37 |
| Europe | Slovakia | 74.25 | 79.57 | 392,704 | 5,465 | 0.0719 | –5.200 | n/a |
| | Russia | 53.46 | 73.75 | 6,288,677 | 146,789 | 0.0428 | –3.056 | 92 |
| Oceania | Fiji* | 75.21 | 71.24 | 30,413 | 905 | 0.0336 | –19.000 | n/a |
| | Palau** | 65.62 | n/a** | 0 | 18 | 0.0000 | –10.286 | n/a |

Due to the absence of the values of the Green Growth Index in the report of the Global Green Growth Institute (2021), this index has been calculated by the author based on the existing data.

* For Palau, the Green Growth Index is calculated in the following way: $(74.19 + 71.24)/2 = 75.21$.

** For Fiji, the Green Growth Index is calculated in the following way: $(68.44 + 66.72 + 61.70)/3 = 65.62$.

n/a – no data in the source. To deal with the gaps in the data, these cells shall be assigned zero values during automatic econometric analysis.

Source: Compiled by the author based on Global Green Growth Institute (2021), Institute of Scientific Communications (2021), International Monetary

**Table 6** Measures of fighting the pandemic and crisis in emerging market economies in 2020

| | | Coronavirus (COVID-19) Testing (ts) | Population with household expenditures on health >25% of total household expenditure or incomer (%) (he) | Share of adults worldwide who agree business has a responsibility to ensure workers and the community are protected from COVID-19 in March 2020, by country (pp) | Value of COVID-19 fiscal stimulus packages in G20 countries as of May 2020, as a share of GDP (Ac) | Density of medical doctors (per 10 000 population) (dc) | Density of nursing and midwifery personnel (per 10 000 population) (md) | Average of 13 International Health Regulations core capacity score (sn) | Total net official development assistance to medical research and basic health sectors per capita (US$), by the recipient country (fn) | Share of people vaccinated against COVID-19, % (vc) | Expand eldercare, childcare and healthcare infrastructure and innovation for the benefit of people and the economy, points 1–100 (sc) |
|---|---|---|---|---|---|---|---|---|---|---|---|
| Africa | South Africa | 1,864.1 | 0.1 | 80 | n/a | 9.1 | 13.1 | 70 | 2.59 | 4.78 | n/a |
| | Kenya | 191.3 | 1.5 | n/a | n/a | 1.6 | 11.7 | 43 | 3.42 | 1.23 | n/a |
| America | Mexico | 641.1 | 0.2 | n/a | 0.7 | 23.8 | 24.0 | 83 | 0.02 | 20.00 | 36.1 |
| | Brazil | 4,316.3 | n/a | 85 | 8.0 | 21.6 | 101.2 | 87 | 0.04 | 19.52 | n/a |

**Table 6** (cont.)

| | | | | | | | | | | | |
|---|---|---|---|---|---|---|---|---|---|---|---|
| Asia | China* | 90,410.0 | 5.4 | n/a | 2.5 | 19.8 | 26.6 | 93 | 0.06 | 29.99 | n/a |
| | India | 10,211.1 | 3.9 | n/a | 3.5 | 8.6 | 17.3 | 78 | 0.18 | 7.55 | n/a |
| Europe | Slovakia | 219.3 | 0.4 | n/a | n/a | 34.2 | 3.2 | 73 | n/a | 35 | 35.5 |
| | Russia | 21,537.8 | 0.6 | n/a | 2.9 | 37.5 | 85.4 | 99 | n/a | 17.45 | n/a |
| Oceania | Fiji | 4.0 | n/a | n/a | n/a | 8.6 | 33.8 | n/a | 8.56 | 10.85 | n/a |
| | Palau | n/a | n/a | n/a | n/a | 14.2 | 72.6 | 63 | 4.94 | n/a | n/a |

* Due to the absence of the values of the share of the population vaccinated against COVID-19 in the materials of Our World in Data (2021), this share has been calculated by the author based on the existing data (422 million vaccinated people in China and China's population from Table 6: 1,408,095,000 people): 422,000,000*100%/1,408,095,000=29.99%.

** n/a – no data in the source. To deal with the gaps in the data, these cells shall be assigned zero values during automatic econometric analysis.

**Source:** Compiled by the author based on Institute of Scientific Communications (2021d), Our World in Data (2021), World Economic Forum (2021)

## 2.4 Results

### 2.4.1 Modelling of the Impact of the COVID-19 Crisis on Sustainable Development and the Green Economy in Emerging Market Economies

To test hypothesis $H_1$, let us perform the modelling of the impact of the COVID-19 crisis on sustainable development and the green economy in emerging market economies in 2020–1. Based on the data from Table 7, the research model (1) is specified through the following equations of multiple linear regression:

- $GG = 49.54 + 106.79 * cs - 1.01 * eg - 0.09 * si$. Multiple correlations equal 61.39% (moderate), which is a sign of a rather close connection between the indicators in the regression model. According to the obtained model, the Green Growth Index changes in the following ways. (1) In case of an increase in COVID-19 cases by 1 per 1 million people, it grows by 106.79 points (contradictory – relatively positive impact but with a negative qualitative treatment). (2) In case of acceleration of the rate of economic growth in 2020 by 1%, it decreases by 1.01 points (contradictory – relatively negative impact since the growth rate in 2020 was negative; therefore, qualitative treatment could be positive and negative). (3) In case of growth of the self-isolation index by 1 point, it decreases by 0.09 points (negative impact).
- $SD = 54.98 + 349.99 * cs + 0.93 * eg + 0.06 * si$. Multiple correlations equal 55.89% (moderate), which is a sign of a rather close connection between the indicators in the regression model. According to the obtained model, the SDI changes in the following ways. (1) In case of an increase in COVID-19 cases by 1 per 1 million people, it grows by 349.99 points (contradictory – relatively positive impact but with negative qualitative treatment). (2) In case of acceleration of the rate of economic growth in 2020 by 1%, it grows by 0.93 points (contradictory – relatively positive impact since the growth rate in 2020 was negative; therefore, qualitative treatment could be positive and negative). (3) In case of growth of the self-isolation index by 1 point, it grows by 0.06 points (positive influence).

The results of the modelling of the impact of the COVID-19 crisis on sustainable development and the green economy in emerging market economies in 2020–1 demonstrate that the rate of economic growth (reduction of gross domestic product (GDP)) and self-isolation (lockdown) had opposite effects on the green economy (a negative sign of the regression coefficients) and sustainable development (a positive sign of the regression coefficients). Since self-isolation is the most manageable variable among the selected factor variables, which are differentiated for the studied results, let us compile two

**Table 7** Correlation analysis and calculation of weight coefficients

| Variable | Correlation with GG, % | Correlation with SD, % | Sum of correlation coefficients that demonstrate a positive connection between the indicators (with GG and SD at the same time) | Weight coefficients |
|---|---|---|---|---|
| ts | −5.52 | 20.52 | 20.52 | 0.05 |
| he | −35.33 | 15.09 | 35.33 | 0.09 |
| pp | −23.15 | 12.79 | 12.79 | 0.03 |
| ac | −25.71 | 24.51 | 24.51 | 0.06 |
| dc | 41.69 | 32.74 | 74.43 | 0.19 |
| md | 6.02 | −25.99 | 6.02 | 0.02 |
| sn | −29.1 | 11.62 | 11.62 | 0.03 |
| fn | 31.96 | −38.52 | 31.96 | 0.08 |
| vc | 46.79 | 62.68 | 109.47 | 0.27 |
| sc | 45.21 | 28.26 | 73.47 | 0.18 |
| Sum for the column | - | - | 400.13 | 1.00 |

**Source:** Author

scenarios – depending on the level – which reflect the alternative variant of the course of the COVID-19 pandemic and crisis from the positions of the green economy and sustainable development in emerging market economies.

The scenario of sustainable development envisages total self-isolation (an increase of the self-isolation index up to 90 points). The scenario of green growth considers the refusal from self-isolation (decrease of the self-isolation index down to 5 points). Since regression of both resulting variables with the number of COVID-19 cases has the positive sign and the fight against the viral threat is directly opposite to the idea of the growth of the number of cases (aimed at its reduction), this indicator remains unchanged in both scenarios (at the level of 2021: 0.03 per 1 million people). To forecast the most probable rate of economic growth for both scenarios, a regression curve which reflects the dependence of GDP growth rate on the self-isolation index is built (Figure 4).

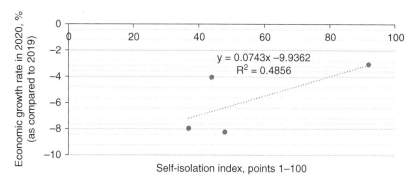

**Figure 4** Regression curve reflecting the dependence of economic growth rate on the self-isolation index in emerging market economies in 2020–1. *Source*: Author

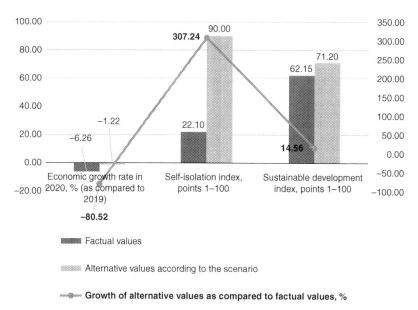

**Figure 5** The scenario of sustainable development – total self-isolation in emerging market economies in 2020–1. *Source*: Author

According to the regression curve (Figure 4), an increase of the self-isolation index by 1 point in emerging market economies in 2020–1 leads to an increase of economic growth rate by 0.0743% per year. The results of the scenario analysis are given in Figures 5 and 6.

According to Figure 5, the scenario of sustainable development – total self-isolation in emerging market economies in 2020–1 – would have allowed

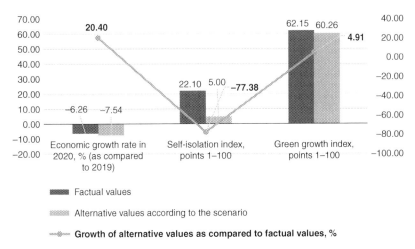

**Figure 6** The scenario of green growth: refusal from self-isolation in emerging market economies in 2020–1. *Source*: Author

reducing (by 80.52%) the decrease of the economic growth rate from factual (in 2020) 6.26% to 1.22%, as well as increasing the SDI from factual 62.15 points to 71.20 points – that is, by 14.56%.

According to Figure 6, the scenario of green growth refusal from self-isolation in emerging market economies in 2020–1 would have led to a deeper (by 20.40%) reduction of economic growth rate (7.54%), which would have ensured an increase of the Green Growth Index (by 4.91%) from factual 62.15 points to 60.26 points.

### 2.4.2 Assessment of the Consequences of Implementing the Measures of Fighting the Pandemic and Crisis in Emerging Market Economies in 2020 for the Green Economy and Sustainable Development

In order to assess in the most precise manner the consequences of implementing anti-crisis in emerging market economies in 2020 for the green economy and sustainable development, the correlation analysis of the connection between the implemented measures from Table 8 and the results (GG and SD) from Table 7 are depicted in Table 9.

In Table 7, the greyed areas show the correlation coefficients with a positive connection between the indicators. Also, the sum of correlation coefficients that demonstrate the positive connection between the indicators (with GG and SD at the same time) is calculated. Based on this, the weight coefficients are obtained in the following way. For example, the weight coefficient for ts: $20.52/400.13 = 0.05$ (sum for all weight coefficients equals 1).

**Table 8** Systemic evaluation of the consequences of implementing anti-pandemic measures in emerging market economies in 2020 for the green economy and sustainable development

| Indicator | Arithmetic mean for the sample | Best value | Ratio to the best value, points 1–100 | Weight coefficient | Weighted sum |
|---|---|---|---|---|---|
| COVID-19 tests | 12,939.50 | 90,410* | 14.31 | 0.05 | 0.72 |
| Population with household expenditures on health >25% of total household expenditure or incomer, %*** | 1.21 | 5.4** | 77.59 | 0.09 | 6.98 |
| Share of adults worldwide who agree business has a responsibility to ensure workers and the community are protected from COVID-19 in March 2020, by country, % | 16.50 | 100.00 | 16.50 | 0.03 | 0.50 |
| Value of COVID-19 fiscal stimulus packages in Group of 20 (G20) countries as of May 2020, as a share of GDP | 1.76 | 8* | 22.00 | 0.06 | 1.32 |
| Density of medical doctors (per 10,000 population) | 17.90 | 37.5* | 47.73 | 0.19 | 9.07 |
| Density of nursing and midwifery personnel (per 10,000 population) | 38.89 | 101.2* | 38.43 | 0.02 | 0.77 |
| Sanitary level, points 1–100 | 68.90 | 100.00 | 68.90 | 0.03 | 2.07 |
| Total net official development assistance to medical research and basic health sectors per capita (US$), by the recipient country | 1.98 | 8.56* | 23.14 | 0.08 | 1.85 |
| Share of people vaccinated against COVID-19, % | 14.64 | 100.00 | 14.64 | 0.27 | 3.95 |
| Expand eldercare, childcare, and healthcare infrastructure and innovation for the benefit of people and the economy, points 1–100 | 7.16 | 100.00 | 7.16 | 0.18 | 1.29 |

\*   The best (maximum) value for the sample

\*\*   The worst (minimum) value for the sample

\*\*\*  Indicator, for which the rule 'the lower, the better' is applied

**Source:** Author

Based on the weight coefficients obtained, Saaty's method is used (Table 8) to perform a systemic evaluation of the consequences of implementing anti-pandemic measures in emerging market economies in 2020 for the green economy and sustainable development.

According to Table 8, the systemic measuring (hierarchy synthesis) of the consequences of implementing anti-pandemic measures in emerging market economies in 2020 for the green economy and sustainable development is the sum of weighted sums from Table 8: $0.72 + 6.98 + 0.50 + 1.32 + 9.07 + 0.77 + 2.07 + 1.85 + 3.95 + 1.29 = 28.51$.

The obtained systemic measuring is a sign of a small contribution ($28.51 < 40$) and the insufficient consideration of the interests of the green economy and sustainable development during the implementation of economic crisis management measures and anti-pandemic measures.

### 2.4.3 Case Study of the Impact of the COVID-19 Crisis on Sustainable Development and the Green Economy in Emerging Market Economies by the Example of Russia in 2020–1

In June 2021, Accenture, the European Business Association, the Russian–German Chamber of Commerce, the Russian Union of Industrialists and Entrepreneurs, and the Embassy of the Federal Republic of Germany in Russia presented the results of a joint sociological survey conducted among the representatives of thirteen spheres of the Russian economy in 2020–1 (RBC, 2021). This survey showed that 98% of Russian companies consider the Environmental, Social and Governance Agenda (ESG Agenda) (the issues of the green economy and sustainable development) to be of top priority for the economy overall and for these companies in particular. However, only 66% of Russian companies have successfully integrated the ESG agenda into their activities.

The largest interest in the ESG Agenda among Russian companies is observed in machine-building and other industrial enterprises (82%), trade companies (75%), food industry companies (73%), and financial sector companies (71%). The key drivers of the ESG Agenda, according to Russian companies, are as follows:

- Green reorientation of the investment flows
- Growth of the requirements of consumers (and society) for corporate social responsibility and the contribution to implementing the SDGs from business (51%)
- Outlining green market trends and growth of green competition (44%)
- Increase of pressure from government and supranational regulators (41%).

The respondents also observed that the pandemic was a serious stimulus for the more active implementation of the ESG Agenda (28%).

The National Research University Higher School of Economics (2021) notes that the pandemic stimulated the creation of responsible communities and green cities in Russia in 2020–1. A notable example is Moscow, which successfully implemented a special territorial approach to the achievement of the SDGs that stimulates the growth of quality of life and the inflow of green investments, as well as wide dissemination of and support for the ESG Agenda in the business sphere.

## 2.5 Conclusion

The results of this study demonstrate the specifics of the impact of the COVID-19 crisis on sustainable development and the green economy in emerging market economies, which reside, firstly, in the fact that the green economy cannot be associated with sustainable development in these countries. Amid the COVID-19 pandemic, the rate of economic growth (reduction of GDP) had an opposite impact on the green economy (an increase of economic growth rate in 2020 by 1% lead to its decrease by 1.01 points) and sustainable development (an increase of economic growth rate in 2020 by 1% lead to its increase by 0.93 points). There are also differences in the influence of self-isolation on the green economy (growth of the self-isolation index by 1 point lead to its decrease by 0.09 points) and sustainable development (growth of the self-isolation index by 1 point lead to its increase by 0.06 points).

Contrary to the experience of advanced market economies and to existing belief, it has been determined that self-isolation does not hinder but stimulates economic growth, allowing the overcoming of not only the pandemic but also the economic crisis caused by COVID-19. Taking into account the results of the economic and mathematical modelling of the impact of the COVID-19 crisis on sustainable development and the green economy in emerging market economies, the scenarios reflecting the alternative consequences of the COVID-19 pandemic for the green economy and sustainable development, depending on the change of the influence of the crisis factors on them, have been compiled.

The first scenario, that of sustainable development, envisages total self-isolation in emerging market economies in 2020–1. It would have allowed slowing the reduction of economic growth rate by 80.52% from the 2020 value of 6.26% down to 1.22% and increasing (by 14.56%) the SDI from a factual 62.15 points up to 71.20 points.

The second scenario, that of green growth, means a refusal of self-isolation in emerging market economies in 2020–1. This scenario would have led to a larger (by 20.40%) decrease of economic growth rate of 7.54% but to an increase of the Green Growth Index (by 4.91%) from a factual 62.15 points to 60.26 points. These scenarios clearly show and emphasize the contradiction between the green economy and sustainable development in emerging market economies, which proves hypothesis $H_1$.

Secondly, the determined specifics are as follows: the contribution of the 2020 measures of the fight against the pandemic in emerging market economies to support the green economy and sustainable development is small (28.51 points out of 100; anything less than 40 points is a critical threshold), which proves hypothesis $H_2$. For the fullest realization of the potential of these measures and the well-balanced approach to the fight against the pandemic, which would ensure economic crisis management (stimulation of economic growth) and support for the green economy and sustainable development at the same time, the following measures are recommended: vaccination (weight coefficient: 0.27), an increased density of doctors (0.19), and expansion of eldercare, childcare, and healthcare infrastructure and innovation for the benefit of people and the economy (0.8).

The Russian case study of the impact of the COVID-19 crisis on sustainable development and the green economy in emerging market economies has demonstrated that the pandemic and crisis stimulated intensive dissemination and support for the ESG Agenda at the level of entrepreneurship (98%), as well as the creation of responsible communities and green cities (e.g., Moscow). The contribution of this research to literature lies in the clarification of the specific nature of the impact of the COVID-19 crisis on sustainable development and the green economy in emerging market economies.

## 3 The COVID-19 Crisis: Potential Harm to Sustainable Development and the Green Economy and Prospects for Mitigating It As a New Challenge for State Management

### 3.1 Introduction

Cyclicity is one of the key features of the modern market economy that should be taken into account during the development and implementation of state management (D'Amato et al., 2017; Heynen et al. 2006). Crises determine a special context of the functioning of economic systems which requires state management measures. An excellent example is the regulation of economic growth (Sosa & Pereira, 2020). At the rise of the economy phase, the most effective policy is free trade, which envisages the absence of government interference with the market mechanism and foreign economic activities (Stanley, 2020).

However, at the economic contraction phase, free trade becomes dangerous since it could increase the scale of overproduction in the economy and reduce the competitiveness of domestic entrepreneurship to an unacceptably low level, depriving the economy of possibilities for further post-crisis restoration. Therefore, in practice, it is often replaced by protectionism or its separate forms, which partially limit the freedom of trade and the market mechanism (Matousek & Rummel, 2020). The anti-crisis effect of protectionism limits the negative influence of external factors on the economy and gives it an opportunity for quick restoration, as well as preserving a competitive environment and business activity at a relatively high level, for further transition to the phase of growth (avoiding stagnation/long crisis) (Goyal & Sergi, 2020).

A new standard of quality of economic growth achieved in the twenty-first century dictates the necessity to support not only a high rate of growth but also progress in the sphere of sustainable development and the green economy. This determines the importance of studying the harm of the COVID-19 crisis to sustainable development and the green economy, which could potentially include, firstly, an increase of environment pollution (slowdown of the rate of implementation or regress on SDG11, SDG12, SDG14, and SDG15) and unfavourable climate change (slowdown of the rate of implementation or regress on SDG13) due to the reduced attention of society, government, and business to the ecological costs of economic growth caused by its critical decrease amid the COVID-19 pandemic (Wamboye, 2021).

Secondly, reduction of the energy efficiency of economy (slowdown of the rate of implementation or regress on SDG7) due to the necessity for restoration of the pre-crisis rate of economic growth in the shortest time possible, with insufficient attention to an increase of economy's energy intensity. Thirdly, growth of unemployment (slowdown of the rate of implementation or regress on SDG8) is a frequent manifestation of economic crises caused by the reduction of business activities (Escribano & Pena, 2021).

The problem is that possible harm to sustainable development and the green economy in 2020 was done not only by the COVID-19 crisis, but also by states' anti-crisis measures. Similar to economic crisis management, ecological and social crisis management could lead to the opposite effect in the conditions of economic contraction and could require special (alternative) measures.

The goal of this section is to study the harm of the COVID-19 crisis and standard anti-crisis measures to sustainable development and the green economy, as well as to develop alternative measures of crisis management, which determine state management's prospects of mitigating the crisis and ensuring an effective reaction to a new challenge.

The novelty of this research resides in proving the ineffectiveness in the emergence of an opposite effect (harm) of standard measures of support to the green economy and sustainable development amid the COVID-19 crisis. For the first time, the harm of the crisis is associated with the harm of the anti-crisis measures supposed to reduce it. The originality of this research is in substantiating the necessity to develop and use special (alternative) measures of support for the green economy and sustainable development amid the COVID-19 crisis, which includes an increase of innovative activity in the economy.

This research is unique in that it investigates the experience of emerging market economies, of which a specific feature (compared to advanced market economies) is the necessity to manifest increased flexibility during the implementation of the anti-crisis measures of the green economy and sustainable development amid the COVID-19 crisis. For emerging market economies, a prospective package of anti-crisis measures is formed and recommendations for their use are offered for the highly effective support of the green economy and sustainable development amid the COVID-19 crisis.

This introduction is followed by a literature review, description of materials and methodology, and the following results:

- modelling sustainable development and the green economy in 2020: harm of the crisis versus harm of the anti-crisis measures
- economic policy implications of mitigating the harm of COVID-19 to sustainable development and the green economy based on a flexible combination of standard and alternative measures
- case study of the use of alternative crisis management measures against COVID-19 using the example of Russia in 2020–1.

## 3.2 Literature Review

All aspects of the potential harm of the COVID-19 crisis to sustainable development and the green economy, which were described in the Introduction, have been examined in detail in the existing literature. Firstly, the issues of environmental pollution amid the COVID-19 crisis have been elaborated in the works of the following authors.

Madineni et al. (2021) concluded that natural processes dominated pollution levels during COVID-19 lockdowns across India. Vasquez-Apestegui et al. (2021) found an association between air pollution in Lima and the high incidence of COVID-19, providing findings from a post hoc analysis. Mo et al. (2021) conducted a cause analysis of PM2.5 pollution during the COVID-19 lockdown in Nanning, China. Dabbour et al. (2021) determined the effect of climatology parameters on air pollution during the COVID-19 pandemic in Jordan. Ye et al. (2021) studied health and related economic benefits associated with the reduction in air pollution during the COVID-19 outbreak in 367 cities in China.

In addition, the issues of climate change amid the COVID-19 crisis were explored by Leal Filho et al. (2021), who studied the impacts of the early onset of the COVID-19 pandemic on climate change research, presenting the implications for policymaking, while Lovejoy (2021) determined the connection between nature, COVID-19, disease prevention, and climate change.

Amnuaylojaroen and Parasin (2021) found an association between COVID-19, air pollution, and climate change, and Borhani et al. (2021) noted the changes in short-lived climate pollutants during the COVID-19 pandemic in Tehran, Iran. Negev et al. (2021) described regional lessons from the COVID-19 outbreak in the Middle East given the transition from infectious diseases to climate change adaptation.

Thirdly, the issues of energy efficiency amid the COVID-19 crisis are analyzed in Popkova and Sergi (2020a), and Jiang et al. (2021) note that energy, environmental, economic, and social equity (4E) are under the pressures of COVID-19 vaccination mismanagement. Jiang et al. (2021) describe the global perspective of this problem. Hartono et al. (2021) determined the effect of COVID-19 on energy consumption and carbon dioxide emissions in Indonesia.

Wang et al. (2021) explored the impact of the COVID-19 pandemic on energy consumption and presented fresh insight into the difference between a pandemic-free scenario and actual electricity consumption in China. Hoang et al. (2021) defined COVID-19 as a driver of the global shift to clean energy, while Rita et al. (2021) describe lockdown era's air pollution impact through the utilization of more renewable energy resources.

Fourthly, the issues of unemployment amid the COVID-19 crisis are investigated in the works of Popkova and Sergi (2021) and Popkova et al. (2020). Mitman and Rabinovich (2021) deem it necessary to extend unemployment benefits amid COVID-19, and Bocchino et al. (2021) explore unemployment during COVID-19 based on a comparison of three population groups.

Davidescu et al. (2021) describe the socio-economic effects of the COVID-19 pandemic and explore uncertainty in the forecast of the Romanian unemployment rate for the period 2020–3. Vijay et al. (2021) study a period from a recession to the COVID-19 pandemic and perform an inflation–unemployment comparison between the UK and India. Svabova et al. (2021) evaluate the impacts of the COVID-19 pandemic on the development of the unemployment rate in Slovakia with a counterfactual before-and-after comparison.

This review reveals serious shortcomings in the existing literature of insufficient attention to the special context of the COVID-19 pandemic and orientation at standard measures of support for the green economy and sustainable development. This, similarly to the measures of support for economic growth, might prove ineffective or harmful in a new context. Furthermore, the following research gaps were identified.

The first gap is the insufficient scientific elaboration of the measures of support for the green economy and sustainable development amid the COVID-19 pandemic and crisis. The practical experience of using the standard measures of this support has been poorly studied and requires further research.

The second gap is uncertainty on alternative (special) measures of support for the green economy and sustainable development amid the COVID-19 pandemic and crisis. This leads to the forced use of standard measures, even if their ineffectiveness amid the COVID-19 pandemic and crisis is proved, due to the absence of an alternative that is scientifically substantiated. This underscores the need for further studies and experiments aimed at the search for special measures of crisis management of the green economy and sustainable development.

The third gap is insufficient attention to the experience of emerging market economies. Studies on the experience of advanced market economies are predominant in the existing literature and are the basis for determining the harm of the COVID-19 crisis to sustainable development and the green economy. The specifics of emerging market economies could lead to uncharacteristic (not typical for advanced market economies) manifestation of the harm of the COVID-19 crisis and anti-crisis measures to sustainable development and the green economy.

This research aims to fill these gaps and to overcome the shortcomings in the existing literature.

## 3.3 Materials and Method

### 3.3.1 Research Hypotheses

This study is based on hypothetical and deductive principles. Two hypotheses are used:

Hypothesis $H_1$: Amid the COVID-19 crisis, the standard (due to ineffectiveness or even harm) measures of support for the green economy and sustainable development (at least some of the following conditions should be met) should not be used:

- State requirements and standards of environment protection (a 'narrow' measure of state management) do not reduce environment pollution and do not stop unfavourable climate change.

- Regulation of energy efficiency (a 'narrow' measure of state management) does not stimulate the improvement of the energy trilemma.
- Protected employment (a 'narrow' measure of state management) does not reduce unemployment.
- Corporate social responsibility (as a universal, 'wide' measure of corporate management) does not reduce environmental pollution, does not stop unfavourable climate change, does not stimulate the improvement of the energy trilemma, and does not reduce unemployment.

Hypothesis $H_2$: Amid the COVID-19 crisis, a prospective special (alternative) measure of support for the green economy and sustainable development is an increase of the innovative activity in the economy, which allows replacing standard measures where they cannot be applied and allows ensuring a striking anti-crisis effect.

### 3.3.2 Methodology and Empirical Data

The methodology of this research is based on regression analysis, a precise and reliable method of economic statistics. To test hypothesis $H_1$, we determine regression dependencies of the consequences of the COVID-19 crisis' impact on the results in the sphere of sustainable development and the green economy – on SDG11, SDG12, SDG14, and SDG15 (growth of the pollution index, PL); SDG13 (growth of the climate index, CC); SDG7 (growth of the energy trilemma index, EE); and SDG8 (growth of unemployment, UE) – on standard measures:

- State requirements and standards of environment protection (a 'narrow' measure of state management, re)
- Regulation of energy efficiency (a 'narrow' measure of state management, ev)
- Protected employment (a 'narrow' measure of state management, se)
- Corporate social responsibility (as a universal, 'wide' measure of corporate management, csr).

The research models for testing hypothesis $H_1$ are:

$$\begin{cases} PL = a_{pl} + b_{pl1} * re + b_{pl2} * csr; \\ CC = a_{cc} + b_{cc1} * re + b_{cc2} * csr; \\ EE = a_{ee} + b_{ee1} * ev + b_{ee2} * csr; \\ UE = a_{ue} + b_{ue1} * se + b_{ue2} * csr. \end{cases} \tag{8}$$

The logic of testing hypothesis $H_1$ is that at least certain regression coefficients in the research models have to conform to the following conditions:

$b_{pl1} > 0$, $b_{pl2} > 0$, $b_{cc1} < 0$, $b_{cc2} < 0$, $b_{ee1} < 0$, $b_{ee2} < 0$, $b_{ue1} > 0$, $b_{ue2} > 0$. These conditions characterize the negative influence of the crisis management measures on the results in the sphere of sustainable development and the green economy.

To obtain the correct data, a representative sample was formed from emerging market economies of different regions of the world. Australia and Oceania are not included in the sample since there are no statistical data for the selected indicators. The empirical basis of the research is presented in Tables 9–11.

As shown in Table 9, the arithmetic mean of the pollution index in 2020 was 58.69 points. Its growth compared to 2019 (58.60 points) is 0.15%. An increase in environmental pollution is a sign of the negative influence of the COVID-19 crisis on the green economy and sustainable development; therefore, crisis management measures are needed.

The arithmetic mean of the climate index in 2020 was 76.40 points. Its growth compared to 2019 (74.63 points) is 2.37%. An increase in climate favourability is a sign of the positive influence of the COVID-19 crisis on the green economy and sustainable development; therefore, crisis management measures are not needed.

As shown in Table 10, the arithmetic mean of the energy trilemma index was 69.71 points in 2020. Its growth compared to 2019 (67.84 points) was 2.75%. The growth of energy efficiency demonstrates a positive influence of the COVID-19 crisis on the green economy and sustainable development, so crisis management measures are not needed.

The arithmetic mean of unemployment was 9.20% in 2020. Its growth compared to 2019 (10.94%) was 18.95%. The growth of unemployment demonstrates a negative influence of the COVID-19 crisis on sustainable development, so crisis management measures are needed.

In order to test hypothesis $H_2$, the regression dependence of the consequences of the influence of the COVID-19 crisis on the results in the sphere of sustainable development and the green economy (PL, CC), EE and UE) on the special (alternative) measure – increase of innovative activity in economy (iv) – is determined. The research models for testing hypothesis $H_2$ have the following form:

$$\begin{cases} PL = a_{pl2} + b_{pl3} * dg; \\ CC = a_{cc2} + b_{cc3} * dg; \\ EE = a_{ee2} + b_{ee3} * dg; \\ UE = a_{ue2} + b_{ue3} * dg. \end{cases} \qquad (9)$$

Hypothesis $H_2$ is proven if $b_{pl3} < 0$ and/or $b_{cc3} > 0$ and/or $b_{ee3} > 0$ and/or $b_{ue3} < 0$. For qualitative reconsideration of the quantitative results, a Russian

**Table 9** Statistics on environment pollution and climate favourability in countries of the sample in 2019–20 and its growth

| Region of the world | Country | Pollution index, points 1–100 | | | Climate index, points 1–100 | | |
|---|---|---|---|---|---|---|---|
| | | 2019 | 2020 | Growth* (PL), % | 2019 | 2020 | Growth* (CC), % |
| Africa | Morocco | n/a | 70.64 | 0.00 | n/a | 91.70 | 0.00 |
| | Egypt | 86.48 | 85.65 | -0.96 | 91.98 | 91.98 | 0.00 |
| | South Africa | 56.95 | 57.30 | 0.61 | 95.97 | 95.25 | -0.75 |
| America | Chile | 65.54 | 65.78 | 0.37 | 90.21 | 90.21 | 0.00 |
| | Argentina | 52.35 | 50.67 | -3.21 | 98.28 | 98.28 | 0.00 |
| | Brazil | 57.72 | 54.98 | -4.75 | 95.35 | 97.16 | 1.90 |
| Asia | Qatar | 66.48 | 61.06 | -8.15 | 36.03 | 36.03 | 0.00 |
| | Saudi Arabia | 67.26 | 65.09 | -3.23 | 41.42 | 45.98 | 11.01 |
| | Indonesia | 62.78 | 66.56 | 6.02 | 68.96 | 74.15 | 7.53 |
| Europe | Slovakia | 41.89 | 39.66 | -5.32 | 78.13 | 78.13 | 0.00 |
| | Slovenia | 24.33 | 24.06 | -1.11 | 78.08 | 77.56 | -0.67 |
| | Russia | 62.80 | 62.79 | -0.02 | 46.53 | 40.36 | -13.26 |

* Growth in 2020 compared to 2019

n/a – data are absent in the source. To deal with the gaps in the data, these cells are assigned zero values during automatic econometric analysis.

**Source:** Compiled by the author based on Institute of Scientific Communications (2021a)

**Table 10** Statistics on the energy trilemma and unemployment in countries of the sample in 2019–20 and their growth

| Region of the world | Country | Energy trilemma index, points 1–100 | | | Unemployment, % | | |
|---|---|---|---|---|---|---|---|
| | | 2019 | 2020 | Growth[*] (EE), % | 2019 | 2020 | Growth[*] (UE), % |
| Africa | Morocco | 61.1 | 62.8 | 2.78 | 9.200 | 11.900 | 29.35 |
| | Egypt | 59.9 | 59.8 | −0.17 | 8.612 | 8.296 | −3.67 |
| | South Africa | 58.9 | 62.1 | 5.43 | 28.700 | 29.175 | 1.66 |
| America | Chile | 69.4 | 71.7 | 3.31 | 7.223 | 10.778 | 49.22 |
| | Argentina | 72.4 | 73.6 | 1.66 | 9.825 | 11.364 | 15.66 |
| | Brazil | 71.6 | 74.9 | 4.61 | 11.925 | 13.242 | 11.04 |
| Asia | Qatar | 67.9 | 69.1 | 1.77 | n/a | n/a | 0.00 |
| | Saudi Arabia | 62.8 | 67.0 | 6.69 | 5.625 | n/a | 0.00 |
| | Indonesia | 64.1 | 66.8 | 4.21 | 5.280 | 7.070 | 33.90 |
| | Slovakia | 75.6 | 76.7 | 1.46 | 5.758 | 6.675 | 15.93 |
| | Slovenia | 79.2 | 78.2 | −1.26 | 4.433 | 5.132 | 15.77 |
| | Russia | 71.2 | 73.8 | 3.65 | 4.600 | 5.783 | 25.72 |

* Growth in 2020 compared to 2019

n/a – data are absent in the source. To deal with the gaps in the data, these cells are assigned zero values during automatic econometric analysis.

**Source:** Compiled by the author based on Institute of Scientific Communications (2021a), International Monetary Fund (2021), World Energy Council (2021)

**Table 11** The measures of crisis management in countries of the sample in 2020

| Region of the world | Country | 'Narrow' measures of state management | | | 'Wide' measure of corporate management | Special (alternative) measure |
|---|---|---|---|---|---|---|
| | | Regulation of energy efficiency, points 1–100 | Requirements to environment protection, points 1–100 | Share of protected employment, % | Social entrepreneurship index, points 1–100 | Innovation index, points 1–100 |
| | | re | ev | se | csr | iv |
| Africa | Morocco | 55.5 | 83 | 51.2 | 30.938 | 31.63 |
| | Egypt | 61.0 | 72 | 78.7 | 34.634 | 27.47 |
| | South Africa | 76.2 | 83 | 90.3 | 46.878 | 34.04 |
| America | Chile | 59.4 | 83 | 75.9 | 42.830 | 36.64 |
| | Argentina | 34.1 | 79 | 78.5 | 34.607 | 31.95 |
| | Brazil | 51.8 | 86 | 72.4 | 49.027 | 33.82 |
| Asia | Qatar | 39.9 | 69 | 99.9 | 35.030 | 33.86 |
| | Saudi Arabia | 58.8 | 66 | 53.1 | 41.195 | 32.93 |
| | Indonesia | 25.7 | 76 | 52.7 | 45.161 | 29.72 |
| Europe | Slovakia | 82.9 | 86 | 88.0 | 34.700 | 42.05 |
| | Slovenia | 75.1 | 93 | 89.4 | 38.079 | 45.25 |
| | Russia | 59.2 | 66 | 94.6 | 61.147 | 37.62 |

**Source:** Compiled by the author based on IMD (2021), Institute of Scientific Communications (2021a), Institute of Scientific Communications (2021b), and Institute of Scientific Communications (2021c)

case study of the experience of using alternative measures of COVID-19 crisis management in 2020–1 is performed.

## 3.4 Results

### *3.4.1 Modelling of Sustainable Development and the Green Economy in 2020: Harm of Crisis versus Harm of Anti-crisis Measures*

The consequences of the COVID-19 crisis in the sphere of sustainable development and the green economy on standard measures in countries of the sample in 2020 reflect the regression dependencies (see Table 12), which have been determined based on the data from Tables 9 and 10.

In Table 12, the greyed areas show the regression coefficients that demonstrate a negative impact (harm) of the standard measures for the results in the sphere of sustainable development and the green economy in emerging market economies (from the sample) in 2020. The results of the modelling have shown that the harm of the anti-crisis measures could be compared to the harm of the crisis in 2020:

- State requirements and standards of environment protection (a 'narrow' measure of state management) do not reduce environment pollution and do not stop unfavourable climate change.
- Regulation of energy efficiency (a 'narrow' measure of state management) does not stimulate the improvement of the energy trilemma.
- Corporate social responsibility (as a universal, 'wide' measure of corporate management) does not reduce environmental pollution, does not stop unfavourable climate change, and does not reduce unemployment.

**Table 12** Regression dependencies of the consequences of the COVID-19 crisis on the results in the sphere of sustainable development and the green economy on standard measures in countries of the sample in 2020

| Regression statistics | | Regression model | | | |
|---|---|---|---|---|---|
| | | PL | CC | EE | UE |
| Multiple R | | 34.51 | 42.84 | 52.89 | 37.60 |
| Constant (a) | | −12.72 | 17.57 | −1.52 | 20.23 |
| Regression coefficients (b) at | re | - | - | −0.02 | - |
| | ev | 0.06 | −0.06 | - | - |
| | Se | - | - | - | −0.31 |
| | csr | 0.15 | −0.30 | 0.14 | 0.48 |

**Source:** Author

Therefore, the harm of anti-crisis measures to the green economy and sustainable development is very clear and rather large, proving hypothesis $H_1$. However, there are also positive effects of the anti-crisis measures. Thus corporate social responsibility stimulates the improvement of the energy trilemma and protected employment (a 'narrow' measure of state management) reduces unemployment.

### 3.4.2 Economic Policy Implications to Mitigate the Harm of COVID-19 to Sustainable Development and the Green Economy Based on a Flexible Combination of Standard and Alternative Measures

To determine the expedience of an increase of innovative activity in the economy – as a special (alternative) measure of crisis management of the green economy and sustainable development in the conditions of COVID-19 – a regression analysis of the dependence of the results from Tables 9 and 10 on innovative activity in economy from Table 11 is performed. As a result, it is determined that the use of the considered alternative measure stimulates the improvement of only one result – the reduction of environmental pollution. The determined dependencies of the results in the sphere of sustainable development and the green economy on the effective standard and alternative are demonstrated, in a systemic way, through the regression curves in Figure 7.

As shown in Figure 7, a 1-point increase of innovative activity in the economy leads to a decrease of the pollution index by 0.1702 points. A 1-point increase of the social entrepreneurship index (corporate social responsibility) leads to an increase of the energy trilemma index by 0.1358 points. An increase of the share of protected employment by 1% leads to a decrease of unemployment by 0.2658%. Based on the determined regression dependencies, to mitigate the harm of COVID-19 to sustainable development and the green economy using a flexible combination of the standard and alternative measures, the following economic policy implications are offered:

- Increase of innovative activity in the economy from 34.75 points in 2020 to 100 points (+187.78%)
- Increase of the social entrepreneurship index (corporate social responsibility) from 41.19 points in 2020 to 100 points (+142.80%)
- Growth of the share of protected employment from 77.06% in 2020 to 100% (+29.77%).

The practical implementation of the developed recommendations will ensure the following advantages for the green economy and sustainable development, as seen in Figure 8.

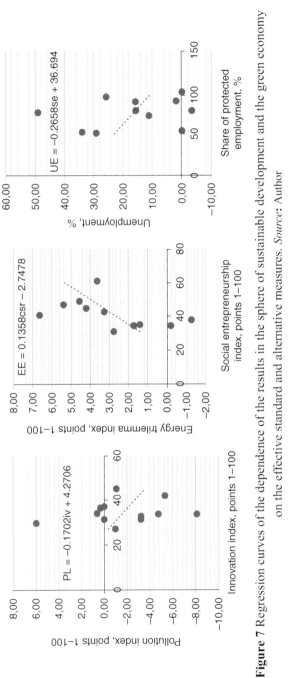

**Figure 7** Regression curves of the dependence of the results in the sphere of sustainable development and the green economy on the effective standard and alternative measures. *Source*: Author

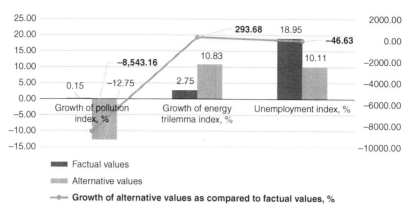

**Figure 8** Advantages of a flexible combination of the standard and alternative measures of management to mitigate the harm of COVID-19 to sustainable development and the green economy *Source*: Author

As shown in Figure 8, the advantages of a flexible combination of the standard and alternative measures of management to mitigate the harm of COVID-19 to sustainable development and the green economy are:

- Negative growth of the pollution index (−12.75%)
- Increase of the growth of the energy trilemma index from 2.85% to 10.83% (by 3.8 times)
- Lower growth of unemployment (10.11% instead of factual 16.21% in 2020).

### 3.4.3 Russian Case Study of Using Alternative Crisis Management Measures during the COVID-19 Pandemic

The successful transformation of state management of the green economy and sustainable development amid the COVID-19 crisis in 2020–1 was demonstrated by Russia. Moscow (4.957 points) entered the top three of innovation ranking and has an important position in the global map of innovative solutions of the fight against COVID-19 (StartupBlink & UNAIDS, 2021). The significant prospective alternative measures of COVID-19 crisis management are 46 projects that were successfully implemented in Russia in 2020, which include the following:

- aervice for automatic monitoring and quantitative measuring of self-isolation (activity of pedestrian and car traffic) with the help of the Yandex Maps app
- Sber app for voice recognition of COVID-19

- a platform for telemedicine Invitro, free virtual consultations DocDoc, online chat with doctors SmartMed and MMT, online testing of the COVID-19 symptoms with the help of AI in the Scanderm and TelePat LLC apps and COVID-19 chatbot Doctis
- online university for advanced training and supporting remote employment Skillbox
- multiple high-precision test sets (with home delivery and quick result) and vaccines
- digital passes with QR codes and diagnostics systems – for example, Neurobotics – robots for tracking contacts at the workplace and Information City – tracking movements in the city and observation of the self-isolation regime
- solutions for 3D bioprinting, which allows accelerating the testing of medicines for the treatment of COVID-19
- artificial intelligence (AI) used for the recognition of COVID pneumonia – Gammamed Group of Companies and prognostic analytics – K-Sky, the systems of AI screening and AI monitoring.

The applied solutions, which were developed and applied in Russia, are universal and could be useful in other countries around the world.

## 3.5 Conclusion

The results of this research have proved hypothesis $H_1$, that not only the crisis but also the anti-crisis measures harmed sustainable development and the green economy in emerging market economies in 2020. Firstly, environmental pollution, under the negative impact of the COVID-19 crisis, grew by 0.15%. An increase of state requirements (and standards) on environment protection (a 'narrow' measure of state management) by 1 point led to an increase of environment pollution (contrary to expectations) by 0.06 points. The growth of corporate social responsibility by 1 point led to an increase of environmental pollution by 0.15 points.

Secondly, the favourability of climate amid the COVID-19 crisis grew by 2.37%. Though the impact of the crisis was positive and the measures of crisis management were not needed, their application could lead to an opposite effect. Thirdly, energy efficiency grew by 3.65%. Though the influence of the crisis is positive and the measures of crisis management are not needed, increased activity of the energy efficiency regulation (a 'narrow' measure of state management) by 1 point led to a decrease of the energy trilemma index by 0.02 points.

Fourthly, unemployment, under the influence of the COVID-19 crisis in emerging market economies, grew by 18.95%. The growth of corporate social responsibility by 1 point led to an increase of unemployment by 0.48%, instead of an expected decrease. Only two of the four considered standard measures of crisis management were effective amid the COVID-19 crisis. Corporate social responsibility contributed to energy efficiency and the fight against unemployment, thereby protecting employment.

Hypothesis $H_2$ has also been proved; the expedience of increasing innovative activity in the economy as a special (alternative) measure of crisis management of the green economy and sustainable development amid the COVID-19 pandemic and crisis has been substantiated. In the sphere of production waste reduction, where neither of the standard measures was applicable, the offered alternative measure has demonstrated a positive effect. The growth of innovative activity in the economy by 1 point led to a reduction of environmental pollution by 0.17 points.

To reach the highest efficiency, it is recommended to use a flexible combination of standard and alternative measures of management in order to mitigate the harm of COVID-19 to sustainable development and the green economy. In case of the maximum use of all three offered measures (an increase of the innovative activity in the economy by 187.78%, increase of corporate social responsibility by 142.80% and increase of the share of protected employment by 29.77%), the following advantages are ensured:

- achievement of the negative growth of the pollution index ($-12.75\%$)
- increase of the growth of the energy trilemma index from 2.85% to 10.83% (by 3.8 times)
- maximization of the positive effect of the COVID-19 crisis
- lower growth of unemployment (10.11% instead of factual 16.21% in 2020).

The case study of the example of Russia in 2020–1 has shown a successful transformation of the practice of state management of the green economy and sustainable development based on the use of alternative measures (innovative projects) of crisis management amid the COVID-19 crisis in 2020–1.

However, it should be noted that there is no positive effect for the fight against climate change from the use of standard or alternative measures of crisis management, which is a limitation of this research. Although the climate has not worsened in the conditions of the COVID-19 pandemic and crisis but, on the contrary, has become better, this might not be the case during future crises. Hence further scientific studies should be undertaken in the search for prospective measures of the fight against climate change that would be effective during crises.

# 4 Scenarios of Sustainable Development of Emerging Market Economies amid the COVID-19 Crisis and Prospects for the Green Economy's Anti-crisis Management

## 4.1 Introduction

From the position of systems theory, the COVID-19 crisis could be treated as a bifurcation point, a turning point after which the economic conditions change radically. In the first phase (of three) of implementing the SDGs from 2015 to 2020, the effective mechanisms of supporting sustainable development were clearly outlined. The most important forms of support for the SDGs are social (through demand), financial (through investments), and state (through adoption and financing of national strategies of implementing the SDGs) (Sergi et al., 2019).

Lockdown, which was initiated for fighting the viral threat amid the COVID-19 pandemic, demonstrated the disproportion of the support for the SDGs, which increased the imbalance in their practical implementation (Popkova et al., 2020; Popkova & Sergi, 2020a, 2021). Thus the issues of healthcare (SDG3) came to the foreground and the issues of reduction of ethnic (SDG10 – e.g., in the USA) and gender (SDG5 – e.g., in North America and Europe) inequality became more important. A quick leap in the development of distant learning contributed significantly to the implementation of SDG4. To overcome the crisis and accelerate economic growth, many countries actively developed the digital economy (Popkova et al., 2021; Popkova & Sergi, 2020c), which stimulates the implementation of SDG9.

However, the issues of environment protection (SDG11–15), despite their weighty importance, were relegated to the background, facing the deficit of previous mechanisms of support. Based on the existing studies (He et al., 2022; Jin et al., 2021; Mondejar et al., 2021), this section offers a general hypothesis ($H_1$) that environment is the central link of the SDGs' chain and thus the progress of the green economy can ensure the systemic progress in the sphere of sustainable development. The logical substantiation of this hypothesis is based on the fact that a favourable environment and the harmony of society and economy with nature raises the population's quality of life, supporting the implementation of all SDGs.

For example, the development of the green economy allows preventing the emergence and transfer of zoonotic diseases, which are passed from animals to humans. Insufficient protection of the environment is one of the main theories of the emergence of the COVID-19 pandemic. Emerging market economies face the urgent problems of environmental protection since these economies have the highest economic costs of economic growth (Geng et al., 2017; Hsu et al., 2013; Lorek & Spangenberg, 2014).

For example, the Chinese economy, which is developing very intensely and which demonstrated a positive rate of economic growth in 2020 (2.270%) as compared to recession in most countries of the world (International Monetary Fund, 2021), holds the seventy-eighth position for production waste in the world (Pollution Index: 40.56 points) in the ranking by Numbeo (2021).

This predetermines the scientific and practical problem – the COVID-19 crisis increased the risks of sustainable development of emerging market economies and threatened not only the perspectives of the successful implementation of the SDGs by 2030, but also the achieved, in the first phase, progress in their implementation. Thus the following research issues became very actual.

RQ1: What impact did the COVID-19 pandemic have on the green economy, and could this impact be compared to the 2020 economic crisis? As an answer to this question, we offer the sub-hypothesis $H_{11}$, that the COVID-19 pandemic had a far more negative impact on the economy than on the environment, due to which the reduction of economic growth is more substantial than the reduction of the green economy, which even demonstrated growth during the lockdown.

RQ2: What are the scenarios of sustainable development of emerging market economies amid the COVID-19 crisis? As an answer to this question, we offer the sub-hypothesis $H_{12}$, that emerging market economies could move according to the optimistic (acceleration of green growth) scenario but it is less probable amid the COVID-19 crisis as compared to the pessimistic (reduction of green growth) scenario, due to which the green economy requires increased crisis management.

RQ3: What are the prospects of the green economy's anti-crisis management for mitigating the negative impact of the COVID-19 crisis on it in emerging market economies? As an answer to this question, we offer the sub-hypothesis $H_{13}$, that the prospects of the green economy's anti-crisis management for mitigating the negative impact of the COVID-19 crisis on it in emerging market economies are connected to the use of such sources of accelerating its growth as efficient and sustainable resource use, natural capital protection, green economic opportunities, and social inclusion.

This section contains the quantitative and qualitative research of the scenarios of sustainable development of emerging market economies amid the COVID-19 crisis and the scientific substantiation of prospects and development of the applied recommendations for the green economy's anti-crisis management within each scenario. The originality of this research resides in comparison – for the first time – of the rates of economic and green growth in the conditions of the COVID-19 pandemic, which allows seeing the scales of economic and ecological crises.

The novelty of this research lies in the application of the scenario approach to studying the prospects of sustainable development of emerging market economies amid the COVID-19 crisis. This allows increasing the precision of the forecast and providing the fullest information support for managerial decisions, thereby reducing the uncertainty. The uniqueness of this research is in offering applied recommendations in the sphere of the anti-crisis management of sustainable development of emerging market economies amid the COVID-19 crisis based on the acceleration of green growth.

This introduction is followed by the literature review, methodology, and results, which include, in particular, the following: (1) comparison of the impact of the COVID-19 pandemic on economic and green growth in emerging market economies in 2020; (2) scenario analysis of sustainable development of emerging market economies amid the COVID-19 crisis; (3) determination of the prospects and development of recommendations in the sphere of the green economy's anti-crisis management for the COVID-19 crisis management in emerging market economies. Conclusions sum up this section.

## 4.2 Literature Review

This research is based on the fundamental provisions of the systems theory, according to which sustainable development of economic systems depends on the order, the context in which it takes place. The COVID-19 pandemic and crisis caused the change of the previous order, but until the new order is established, the uncertainty and large risks of implementing the SDGs remain. The concept of sustainable development of emerging market economies amid the COVID-19 crisis from the position of systems theory is shown in Figure 9.

The concept in Figure 9 envisages that during the stable and strictly determined previous order, the sustainability (complex results of implementing the SDGs) of emerging market economies was growing in the first phase (of three) of implementing the SDGs (2015–20). The COVID-19 crisis was a 'bifurcation point' – a source of changes under the influence of which a new order has to be established.

In the second phase of implementing the SDGs (2020–5), sustainability amid the COVID-19 crisis is connected to uncertainty – it could grow (attractor $\alpha$) or reduce (attractor $\beta$). The COVID-19 pandemic and crisis have a destabilizing impact on sustainability (increase the probability of attractor $\beta$), and the factors of the green economy have a supportive impact (increase the probability of attractor $\alpha$).

In this section, we aim to test the correctness of the concept in Figure 9 and strengthen its factual basis (evidence confirming or disproving the concept). The current problems and prospects of sustainable development of emerging

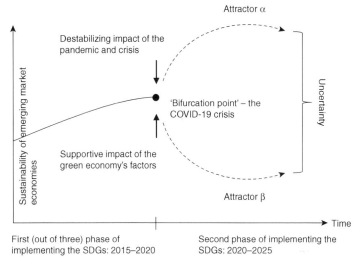

**Figure 9** The concept of sustainable development of emerging market economies amid the COVID-19 crisis from the position of systems theory

*Source*: Author

market economies amid the COVID-19 crisis are studied in detail in the existing literature.

Karmaker et al. (2021) note the improvement of supply chain sustainability in the context of the COVID-19 pandemic in an emerging economy based on exploring drivers using an integrated model. MacGregor Pelikanova et al. (2021) describe small and medium-sized enterprises (SMEs) in the hotel industry addressing the COVID-19 challenges as a Czech sustainability message for emerging economies.

Pereira et al. (2021) study the impact of COVID-19 on emerging economy suppliers and prove the increase in supply chain sustainability. Sardar et al. (2021) prove the impact of ICT on entrepreneurial self-efficacy in the emerging economy and emphasize the necessity to sustain lockdown during the COVID-19 pandemic. Belaid et al. (2021) point out the emerging and advanced economy markets' behaviour during the COVID-19 crisis.

Sriyono et al. (2021) prove the acceleration of performance recovery and competitiveness through non-banking financing in SMEs based on a green economy under the influence of the COVID-19 pandemic. Venter et al. (2021) describe the 'back to nature' tendency, pointing out Norwegians' increased recreational use of urban green space months after the COVID-19 outbreak. Arif et al. (2021) model the COVID-19 and time–frequency connectedness between green and conventional financial markets.

Mayen Huerta and Utomo (2021) prove the association between urban green spaces and subjective well-being in Mexico City during the COVID-19 pandemic. Fasan et al. (2021) perform an empirical analysis and prove that green supply chain management alleviates the effects of COVID-19. Liu et al. (2021) suggest the optimization of healthcare waste management systems based on the green governance principle in the COVID-19 pandemic.

This review reveals that a serious drawback of the existing literature is the use of the previous mechanisms of supporting sustainable development, which were effective before the COVID-19 pandemic and crisis, but which effectiveness and accessibility reduced in the current conditions (new context). Unlike the existing literature sources, this research suggests using new mechanisms of supporting sustainable development which envisage the acceleration of levers for green growth.

Another drawback of the existing literature is the limited ('narrow') description of the prospects of sustainable development of emerging market economies amid the COVID-19 crisis. Some authors treat these prospects positively while others treat them negatively, but the complete picture is not clear. However, this section presents a comprehensive view of the prospects of sustainable development of emerging market economies amid the COVID-19 crisis in considering alternative scenarios.

The problems in the existing literature are, firstly, the insufficient scientific elaboration (uncertainty) of the prospects of sustainable development of emerging market economies amid the COVID-19 crisis. The second problem is the poor elaboration of the contribution of the green economy to sustainable development. These gaps are filled in this research through a deep study and comprehensive consideration of the prospects of sustainable development of emerging market economies amid the COVID-19 crisis, as well as clarification of the contribution of various mechanisms of green growth to sustainable development.

## 4.3 Materials and Methodology

This section uses the following methodology. Firstly, trend analysis is used to determine the impact of the COVID-19 pandemic on the green economy and cyclicity of emerging market economies, the rate of increase in the green growth index (according to Global Green Growth Institute, 2021a, 2021b) and GDP (in constant prices, according to International Monetary Fund, 2021) is calculated for 2020 as compared to 2019.

Secondly, comparative analysis is used to determine the similarities and differences in the increase in economic and green growth. Thirdly, the method of calculation of arithmetic means allows determining the general changes in the rate of economic and green growth for each region of the world and countries of the sample on the whole. The proof of sub-hypothesis $H_{11}$ is the average change of green growth, which has to be positive and/or exceed the average change of economic growth.

To determine scenarios of sustainable development of emerging market economies amid the COVID-19 crisis, a scenario analysis with the Monte Carlo method is performed. Based on the average and standard deviation of the SDI in 2020, a forecast of the change of the index is compiled; 100 random numbers are generated for this and a histogram of their normal distribution is built.

This allows determining the forecast values of the SDI and evaluating the probability of their achievement in practice. The method of trend analysis is used to assess the change of the SDI within each obtained scenario compared to 2020. Sub-hypothesis $H_{12}$ is deemed proved if it is possible to receive alternative scenarios, some of which envisage an increase in the SDI as compared to 2020 and others of which envisage its decrease.

To determine the prospects of the green economy's anti-crisis management to mitigate the negative impact of the COVID-19 crisis on it in emerging market economies, the method of regression analysis is used. It allows, with great precision and correctness, finding the dependence of the SDI on the factors of the green economy:

- efficient and sustainable resource use ($ge_1$)
- natural capital protection ($ge_2$)
- green economic opportunities ($ge_3$)
- social inclusion ($ge_4$).

The formal research model has the following form:

$$SDI = a + b_1 * ge_1 + b_2 * ge_2 + b_3 * ge_3 + b_4 * ge_4 \qquad (10)$$

According to model (10), the SDI is a function of the green economy's factors. Secondly, the least-squares method is used to find the optimal combination of the green economy's factors to mitigate the negative impact (or support the positive impact) of the COVID-19 crisis on it in emerging market economies for each obtained scenario.

Sub-hypothesis $H_{13}$ is deemed proved if there is a positive impact on sustainable development by at least one factor of the green economy and if there is an optimal combination of the green economy's factors to mitigate the negative impact (or support the positive impact) of the COVID-19 crisis on it in emerging market economies for each obtained scenario.

The empirical basis of this research is shown in Table 13. To obtain the most precise and reliable results, the sample includes emerging market economies with different levels of income, of different sizes (length of borders and population), and from different regions of the world.

## 4.4 Results

### 4.4.1 The Impact of the COVID-19 Pandemic on Economic and Green Growth in Emerging Market Economies in 2020

To determine the impact of the COVID-19 pandemic on the green economy and cyclicity of emerging market economies, the rate of growth of the green growth index (according to Table 9) and GDP (in constant prices, according to International Monetary Fund, 2021) is calculated for 2020 as compared to 2019 (Figure 10).

As shown in Figure 10, most emerging market economies display an opposite impact of the COVID-19 pandemic on economic (reduction) and green (increase) growth:

- in Algeria, the decrease of economic growth (−6%) is combined with the growth of the green economy (+25.3%)
- in Tunisia, the decrease of economic growth (−8.8%) is combined with the growth of the green economy (+27.7%)

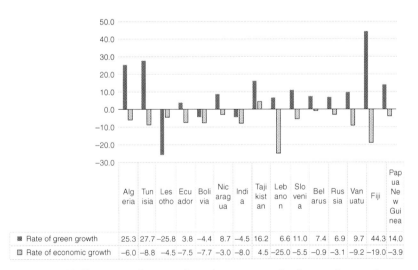

**Figure 10** The rates of economic and green growth of emerging market economies amid the COVID-19 crisis in 2020 as compared to 2019, % *Source:* Calculated and compiled by the author based on International Monetary Fund (2021)

**Table 13** Statistics of sustainable development and the green economy in emerging market economies in 2019–20, points 1–100

| Region of the world | Country | Sustainable Development Index SDI | Efficient and Sustainable Resource Use ge$_1$ | Natural Capital Protection ge$_2$ | Green Economic Opportunities ge$_3$ | Social Inclusion ge$_4$ | Green Growth Index 2020 | Green Growth Index 2019 |
|---|---|---|---|---|---|---|---|---|
| Africa | Algeria | 70.86 | 28.43 | 45.45 | 7.20 | 66.27 | 28.02 | 22.36 |
| | Tunisia | 71.44 | 28.27 | 61.76 | 46.16 | 75.42 | 49.65 | 38.88 |
| | Lesotho | 54.59 | 56.76 | 45.40 | 8.24 | 50.88 | 32.24 | 43.47* |
| America | Ecuador | 72.54 | 60.89 | 70.84 | 20.44 | 75.28 | 50.75 | 48.87 |
| | Bolivia | 67.60 | 55.73 | 69.79 | 14.10 | 68.92 | 44.09 | 46.10 |
| | Nicaragua | 66.29 | 66.11 | 71.45 | 5.12 | 66.42 | 35.60 | 32.74 |
| Asia | India | 60.07 | 41.98 | 55.11 | 30.40 | 51.09 | 43.54 | 45.58 |
| | Tajikistan | 69.76 | 38.45 | 60.85 | 4.17 | 72.86 | 29.04 | 25.00 |
| | Lebanon | 66.84 | 44.09 | 56.10 | 24.49 | 51.56 | 42.04 | 39.45 |
| Europe | Slovenia | 81.60 | 68.36 | 81.85 | 51.34 | 88.53 | 71.01 | 64.00 |
| | Belarus | 78.82 | 57.13 | 72.88 | 15.62 | 83.87 | 48.32 | 45.00 |
| | Russia | 73.75 | 50.55 | 55.84 | 37.17 | 77.88 | 53.46 | 50.00 |

**Table 13** (cont.)

| Region of the world | Country | Sustainable Development Index SDI | Efficient and Sustainable Resource Use ge$_1$ | Natural Capital Protection ge$_2$ | Green Economic Opportunities ge$_3$ | Social Inclusion ge$_4$ | Green Growth Index 2020 | Green Growth Index 2019 |
|---|---|---|---|---|---|---|---|---|
| Oceania | Vanuatu | 60.52 | 80.19 | 64.69 | -** | 32.74 | 59.21* | 53.96* |
| | Fiji | 71.24 | 68.44 | 66.72 | -** | 61.70 | 65.62* | 45.48 |
| | Papua New Guinea | 51.33 | 71.40 | 53.80 | -** | 21.85 | 49.02* | 42.99* |

* Due to the deficit of data in the sources, the following values were calculated by the author:

- Green Growth Index 2020 for Vanuatu = $(80.19 + 64.69 + 32.74)/3 = 59.21$
- Green Growth Index 2020 for Fiji = $(68.44 + 66.72 + 61.70)/3 = 65.62$
- Green Growth Index 2020 for Papua New Guinea = $(71.40 + 53.80 + 21.85)/3 = 49.02$
- Green Growth Index 2019 for Lesotho = $(42.91 + 51.49 + 36.00)/3 = 43.47$
- Green Growth Index 2019 for Vanuatu = $(69.95 + 65.62 + 26.31)/3 = 53.96$
- Green Growth index 2019 for Papua New Guinea = $(58.29 + 59.59 + 11.10)/3 = 42.99$.

** Due to the absence of data in the sources, these cells are assigned zero values during the automatized econometric modelling in order to fill the gaps in the data array.

**Source:** Compiled by the author based on Global Green Growth Institute (2021a, 2021b) and UNDP (2021)

- in Ecuador, the decrease of economic growth (−7.5%) is combined with the growth of the green economy (+3.8%)
- in Nicaragua, the decrease of economic growth (−3%) is combined with the growth of the green economy (+8.7%)
- in Lebanon, the decrease of economic growth (−25%) is combined with the growth of the green economy (+6.6%)
- in Slovenia, the decrease of economic growth (−5.5%) is combined with the growth of the green economy (+11%)
- in Belarus, the decrease of economic growth (−0.9%) is combined with the growth of the green economy (+7.4%)
- in Russia, the decrease of economic growth (−3.1%) is combined with the growth of the green economy (+6.9%)
- in Vanuatu, the decrease of economic growth (−9.2%) is combined with the growth of the green economy (+9.7%)
- in Fiji, the decrease of economic growth (−19%) is combined with the growth of the green economy (+44.3%)
- in Papua New Guinea, the decrease of economic growth (−3.9%) is combined with the growth of the green economy (+14%).

The averaged results for regions of the world and emerging market economies, on the whole, are shown in Figure 11.

As shown in Figure 11, in African countries, the decrease of economic growth (−6.4%) is combined with the growth of the green economy (+9.1%). In countries of America, the decrease of economic growth (−6.1%) is combined

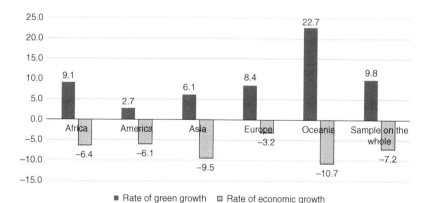

**Figure 11** The rates of economic and green growth of emerging market economies amid the COVID-19 crisis in 2020 as compared to 2019 by regions and for the sample on the whole, % *Source*: Calculated and compiled by the author based on International Monetary Fund (2021)

with the growth of the green economy (+2.7%). In Asian countries, the decrease of economic growth (−9.5%) is combined with the growth of the green economy (+6.1%). In European countries, the decrease of economic growth (−3.2%) is combined with the growth of the green economy (+8.4%). In countries of Oceania, the decrease of economic growth (−10.7%) is combined with the growth of the green economy (+22.7%).

In the full sample of emerging market economies, the comparative analysis has demonstrated the completely different impact of the COVID-19 pandemic on green growth (positive: +9.8%) and on economic growth (negative and less clear: −7.2%). This proves sub-hypothesis $H_{11}$. To determine the progress in the sphere of sustainable development of emerging market economies and the quantitative characteristics of the conceptual model from Figure 9, a trend analysis of the change of the SDI in 2020 (as a result of the first phase of implementing the SDGs) as compared to 2016 (start of the first phase of implementing the SGDs – the first report of the UNDP on sustainable development) is performed (Figure 12).

As shown in Figure 12, there is a positive trend of sustainable development in all emerging market economies. The average growth of the SDI in countries of Africa is 16.83%, in countries of America it is 17.55%, in countries of Asia it is 18.45% and in countries of Europe, it is 8.29%. On average, the growth of the SDI of emerging market economies was 15.28% in 2020 as compared to 2016. That is, at the first phase of implementing the SDGs, the growth of the SDI was 3.82% per year on average.

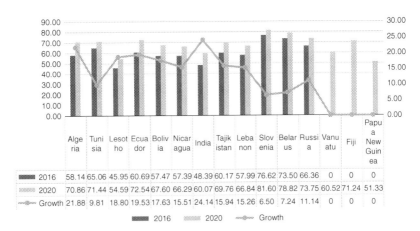

**Figure 12** The SDI of emerging market economies in 2016 and 2020 (in points) and its growth (in %) *Source*: Compiled by the author based on UNDP (2021)

The positive dynamics of the SDI show that the conditions for development were favourable during the first phase of implementing the SDGs. They were the basis for the forecasts of sustainable development at the second phase of implementing the SDGs, compiled before the start of the COVID-19 pandemic. However, the change of the order led to uncertainty, which does not allow using the previously compiled forecasts and predetermines the necessity to compile new forecasts because of the changed context.

### 4.4.2 Scenarios of Sustainable Development of Emerging Market Economies amid the COVID-19 Crisis

To determine the scenarios of sustainable development of emerging market economies amid the COVID-19 crisis, we calculate, based on the data from Table 9, the arithmetic mean (67.82 points) and standard deviation (8.32 points) of the SDI in 2020. Based on the obtained values, 100 random numbers were generated automatically and reflect the forecast of the SDI of emerging market economies amid the COVID-19 crisis. The histogram of the normal distribution of these forecast values is shown in Figure 13.

As shown in Figure 13, the most probable (21% probability) forecast value of the SDI amid the COVID-19 crisis is 70.80 points (the inertial scenario). Most of the other values (total probability $1 + 3 + 4 + 7 + 9 + 17 = 57.38\%$) are below 70.80 points, in the range of 49.11 points to 70.79 points. Since the worst value envisages the reduction of the SDI compared to 2020, this scenario is considered pessimistic. The growth of the SDI within this scenario is from $-27.59\%$ to $4.38\%$.

The remaining values (total probability $\% 12 + 12 + 9 + 5 = 21.62\%$) are above 70.80 points, in the range of 70.81 points to 81.65 points. Since all of these values envisage an increase in the SDI compared to 2020, this scenario is

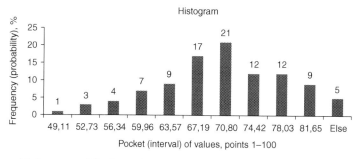

**Figure 13** Forecast of the SDI of emerging market economies amid the COVID-19 crisis *Source*: Author

considered optimistic. The growth of the SDI within this scenario varies from 4.41% to 20.39%. The dynamics of sustainable development of emerging market economies in 2016–20 and the alternative scenarios of future development amid the COVID-19 crisis are shown in Figure 14.

The dynamics (Figure 14) of sustainable development of emerging market economies in 2016–20 and the alternative scenarios of future development amid the COVID-19 crisis confirm the correctness of the concept of sustainable development of emerging market economies amid the COVID-19 crisis from the positions of the systems theory (from Figure 9) and strengthen its factual basis. As shown in Figure 14, the arithmetic mean of the SDI in emerging market economies was 60.64 points in 2016 and by 2020 it had reached 67.82 points. After 2020, amid the COVID-19 crisis, its forecast is in the confidence interval from 49.11 points to 81.65 points. Since the optimistic and pessimistic scenarios were received, sub-hypothesis $H_{12}$ is proved.

### 4.4.3 Prospects and Recommendations in the Sphere of the Green Economy's Anti-crisis Management for Crisis Management of COVID-19 in Emerging Market Economies

To determine the prospects of the green economy's anti-crisis management to mitigate the negative impact of the COVID-19 crisis on it in emerging market economies, we use regression analysis. It shows the following dependence of the SDI on the factors of the green economy (based on the data from Table 9):

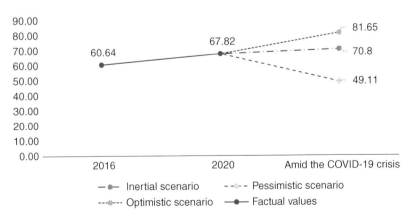

**Figure 14** Dynamics of sustainable development of emerging market economies in 2016–20 and the alternative scenarios of future development amid the COVID-19 crisis, points 1–100 *Source:* Author

$$SDI = 35.27\text{--}0.02 * ge_1 + 1.19 * ge_2 + 0.008 * ge_3 + 0.34 * ge_4 \qquad (2)$$

According to the economic and mathematical model (2), the SDI changes in the following ways:

- Growth of efficiency and sustainability of resource use by 1 point leads to its reduction by 0.02 points.
- Growth of the level of natural capital protection by 1 point leads to its increase by 1.19 points.
- Growth of green economic opportunities by 1 point leads to its increase by 0.008 points.
- Growth of the level of social inclusion by 1 point leads to its increase by 0.34 points.

Multiple correlation equals 92.35% – that is, it is very high, which shows that the change of the green economy's factors by 92.35% explains the change of sustainable development. The standard deviation is small (3.78). To check the reliability of the compiled econometric model, an F test is performed. The value of the F test ($F_{obs}$) equals 14.48. The table value of F criterion ($F_{tabl}$) for fifteen observations and four variables at the significance level 0.05 equals 2.85. Since $F_{obs} > F_{tabl}(14.48 > 2.85)$, the regression model is correct and reliable at the significance level of 0.05.

Thus three out of four factors of green growth ($ge_2$, $ge_3$, and $ge_4$) positively impact the SDI. This opens wide opportunities for optimization – that is, for crisis management of sustainable development in emerging market economies amid COVID-19 based on managing the factors of the green economy.

Based on the obtained econometric model, the least-squares method is used to automatically determine the optimal combination of the factors of the green economy to mitigate the negative impact (or support the positive impact) of the COVID-19 crisis on it in the emerging market economies within each preliminary obtained scenario.

As Table 14 shows, the practical implementation of the inertial scenario needs an increase in the level of natural capital protection up to 65.83 points (by 5.88%), an increase in green economic opportunities up to 17.64 points (by 0.07%), and an increase in the level of social inclusion up to 69.67 points (by 10.56%). This scenario envisages the least increase in green growth among all obtained scenarios.

The practical implementation of the optimistic scenario needs more significant changes: an increase in the level of natural capital protection up to 79.13 points (by 27.28%), an increase in green economic opportunities up to 17.69

**Table 14** Scenarios of sustainable development of emerging market economies amid the COVID-19 crisis

| Characteristics of scenario | | Basic values in 2020 | Inertial scenario | Pessimistic scenario | Optimistic scenario |
|---|---|---|---|---|---|
| Pocket of values of the Sustainable Development Index according to the scenario, points 1–100 | | 67.82 | 70.80 | 49.11–70.79 | 70.81–81.65 |
| Growth of the Sustainable Development Index according to the scenario compared to 2020, % | | - | 4.39 | −27.59–4.38 | 4.41–20.39 |
| Probability of the scenario, % | | - | 21 | 57.38 | 21.62 |
| Recommendations for the green economy's anti-crisis management within the scenario | Natural capital protection | Recommended value, points 1–100 | 62.17 | 65.83 | 95.92 | 79.13 |
| | | Recommended growth, % | - | 5.88 | 54.30 | 27.28 |
| | Green economic opportunities | Recommended value, points 1–100 | 17.63 | 17.64 | 100.00 | 17.69 |
| | | Recommended growth, % | - | 0.07 | 467.21 | 0.34 |
| | Social inclusion | Recommended value, points 1–100 | 63.02 | 69.67 | 96.64 | 93.88 |
| | | Recommended growth, % | - | 10.56 | 53.35 | 48.97 |

**Source:** Author

points (by 0.34%), and an increase in the level of social inclusion up to 93.88 points (by 48.97%).

Prevention of the pessimistic scenario requires more serious managerial measures, which include an increase in the level of natural capital protection up to 95.92 points (by 54.30%), an increase in green economic opportunities up to 100 points (by 467.21%), and an increase in the level of social inclusion up to 96.64 points (by 63.35%).

Thus, for each scenario, we have found the optimal combination of the factors of the green economy to mitigate the negative impact (or support the positive impact) of the COVID-19 crisis on it in emerging market economies. Thus sub-hypothesis $H_{13}$ is proved.

## 4.5 Conclusion

As a result of the research conducted, it is possible to draw the following conclusions. Firstly, measuring and comparative analysis of the impact of the COVID-19 pandemic in emerging market economies in 2020 have shown that the pandemic's impact on green growth is positive (+9.8%) and on economic growth it is negative and less noticeable (−7.2%). Therefore, the pandemic increased the cyclicity of emerging market economies but supported the development of their green economy.

It has also been established that the growth of the SDI of emerging market economies was 15.28% on average in 2020 as compared to 2015. The positive dynamics of the SDI demonstrate the favorability of the conditions for this development during the first phase of implementing the SDGs (2015–20). However, the change of the order under the influence of the COVID-19 pandemic and crisis led to uncertainty, which predetermined the necessity for the compilation of new forecasts because of the changed context.

Secondly, the scenario analysis of sustainable development of emerging market economies amid the COVID-19 crisis has allowed clarifying and quantitatively describing the dynamics of sustainable development of emerging market economies in 2016–20 and determining the alternative scenarios of future development amid the COVID-19 crisis (during the second phase of implementing the SDGs, 2020–5). The obtained results of dynamic modelling and scenario analysis confirm the correctness of the concept of sustainable development of emerging market economies amid the COVID-19 crisis from the position of systems theory and have strengthened its factual basis.

Thirdly, the prospects in the sphere of the green economy's anti-crisis management for the COVID-19 crisis management in emerging market economies have been determined. The inertial scenario reflects the most probable (21% probability) forecast value of the SDI amid the COVID-19 crisis: 70.80 points (growth by 4.39% as compared to 2020). To implement it, it is recommended to raise the level of natural capital protection to 65.83 points (by 5.88%), increase green economic opportunities up to 17.64 points (by 0.07%), and raise the level of social inclusion to 69.67 points (by 10.56%). This scenario envisages the least increase of green growth among all obtained scenarios.

The optimistic scenario unifies the remaining values (total probability – 21.62%) that exceed 70.80 points (in the range from 70.81 points to 81.65 points). The growth of the SDI within this scenario is between 4.41% and 20.39%. To implement it, the more notable changes are recommended: an increase of natural capital protection up to 79.13 points (by 27.28%), an increase of green economic opportunities up to 17.69 points (by 0.34%), and an increase of the level of social inclusion up to 93.88 points (by 48.97%).

The pessimistic scenario includes most of the other values (total probability – 57.38%), which are below 70.80 points (in the range from 49.11 points to 70.79 points). The growth of the SDI within this scenario is in the range −27.59% to 4.38%. For its prevention, we recommend the most serious managerial measures, which include an increase in the level of natural capital protection up to 95.92 points (by 54.30%), an increase in green economic opportunities up to 100 points (by 467.21%), and an increase in the level of social inclusion up to 96.64 points (by 63.35%).

To guarantee successful implementation of the UN global initiative at the second stage of implementing the SDGs (2020–5), it is expedient to use recommendations for the prevention of the pessimistic scenario. After the COVID-19 pandemic and crisis, the scenarios of sustainable development of emerging market economies could be changed, and it is possible to reconsider, according to them, the recommendations on the green economy's anti-crisis management.

The obtained results have proved hypothesis (H$_1$), that the environment is the central link of the SDG chain; thus the progress of the green economy can ensure systemic progress in the sphere of sustainable development.

The contribution of this research to literature are the following:

- reduction of uncertainty as to the prospects of sustainable development of emerging market economies amid the COVID-19 crisis
- substantiation of the contradictory impact of the pandemic on sustainable development with the slowdown of economic growth rate and the increase of cyclicity, combined with the accelerated growth of the green economy
- scientific proof of the substantial contribution of the measures of managing the green economy to the sustainable development of emerging market

economies and development of the applied recommendations on crisis man-agement of sustainable development. This is based on the flexible stimulation of green growth in the three key directions: an increase in the level of natural capital protection, an increase in green economic opportunities, and an increase in the level of social inclusion.

# Conclusion
## Green Economy and Sustainable Development amid the COVID-19 Crisis: Looking into the Future of Emerging Market Economies

Emerging market economies are subjects of the world economy and inter-national relations that especially need support for the SDGs since they are behind developed countries in their implementation. The deep research of the experience of emerging market economies, which was conducted in this Element, demonstrated a range of challenges of the COVID-19 pandemic and crisis to the sustainable development of these countries.

First challenge: Reduced and insufficient support for the green economy. The econometric analysis of statistical data clearly showed the reduction of the volume of green investments (their outflow from developing countries) by almost 12%, reduction of natural capital protection by 5%, and decrease of green trade by 52%. Though the SDI for 2021 (as a result of 2020) is yet to be calculated, it is obvious that it will probably show the negative dynamics.

The problem is not only in regress in implementing the SDGs connected to the development of the green economy – that is, in eliminating the results of the past five years in the sphere of the fight against climate change and preservation of biodiversity, but also in the increased disproportion between results for different SDGs. Thus, for example, significant progress on the global scale has been achieved in the sphere of reduction of gender and ethnic inequality. However, this progress was primarily in developed countries, which increased the disproportion in the implementation of the SDGs between developed and developing countries. This progress also increased the imbalance between the SDGs that are connected to environmental protection and the SDGs that are not based directly on the green economy.

Second challenge: Aggravation of the contradiction between economic growth and the green economy. The economic and mathematical modelling based on an international sample of emerging market economies showed that acceleration of the economic growth rate by 1% in 2020 led to a decrease of the green economy's development by 1.01 points. This is a sign of an exponential increase in the ecological costs of economic growth. Taking into account the fact that they were rather large before this, the post-crisis restoration of the world economy (future economic growth) is a serious threat to the green economy.

In the post-COVID period, there is a risk of destroying all efforts in fighting climate change, such as reduction of waste and preservation of biodiversity in the first five years of implementing the SDGs (2015–20). That is why it is very important to change the approach to the post-crisis restoration of developing countries' economies in the post-COVID period. This restoration must not take place through the depletion of non-renewable resources and their export, together with energy resources, as well as the development of the spheres and companies with low energy efficiency (and high energy intensity) and large production and consumption waste. They should be replaced by responsible production and consumption based on green innovations.

Third challenge: Regress of the green economy. This Element calculates and shows that environmental pollution amid the COVID-19 crisis in 2020 grew by 0.15% as compared to 2019. These are only preliminary data since the main damage to the green economy from the COVID-19 pandemic and crisis is expected to be seen in 2021–2 and maybe even later (delayed effect). A negative signal is a fact that corporate social (ecological) responsibility in emerging market economies amid the COVID-19 pandemic and crisis in 2020 demonstrated idleness in the issue of production waste reduction.

The multiple factor analysis also led to a disappointing result; it was determined that climate change became uncontrolled due to the COVID-19 pandemic and crisis. In the new context, the favourability of climate became independent from standard measures of management – state requirements on environment protection and corporate ecological responsibility – and special (alternative) measures – for example, innovations.

Not only did the measures of management fail to ensure the expected progress in the fight against climate change, but they also led to an opposite effect in the form of aggravation of climate due to their application. The uncontrolled climate change is a delayed-action ecological bomb. A prospective direction for solving this problem is reconstructive land use, which ensures a reversed climate change. Popularization of the reconstructive land use practice is especially required in emerging market economies.

Fourth challenge: Large risks to the green economy's future development. Unfortunately, the results of the forecast show that the pessimistic scenario (57.38%) is most probable in emerging market economies, which envisages the reduction of these countries' sustainable development down to 27.59% (almost by one third as compared to the pre-crisis level) amid the COVID-19 pandemic and crisis. Though the suggested applied recommendations allow avoidance of this negative consequence of the COVID-19 crisis, these above challenges do not allow expectations of significant progress in the development of the green economy in emerging market economies in 2021–2 and possibly after.

However, the development of the green economy offers an effective and systemic answer to the challenges of the COVID-19 pandemic and crisis to sustainable development. Still, there is ambiguity here in that emerging market economies are not similar. Unlike developed countries, which are leaders in almost all international rankings and have similar (close to each other) values of statistical indicators, the scattering of indicator values among emerging market economies is extensive.

The notable regional peculiarities of the green growth emerging market economies were determined. Though this was not specifically researched in this Element, it is possible to suppose the existence of a dependence of the green economy on the level of incomes of emerging market economies. For example, the possibilities of financing green innovations among these countries are strongly differentiated. This requires the reconsideration of the existing categories of countries of the world.

The previous system of categories – with the designation of only developed and developing countries – has become obsolete and does not reflect the modern situation in the world economy. There is a necessity for several subcategories for emerging market economies. Underrun from developed countries is no longer a universal criterion. There are rapidly growing and actively developing economies in Brazil, Russia, India, China, and South Africa (BRICS), which have leading positions in international rankings, together with developed countries.

In addition it is possible to distinguish emerging market economies that have selected their way of development and follow it. They are behind other countries by certain indicators but exceed their rivals by other indicators. Thus certain countries of South America and Africa demonstrate a low rate of economic growth and living standards but outstanding ecological and well-being indicators.

An example is the leadership of Kenya (first position, 99.79 points), Costa Rica (second position, 99.48 points), Argentina (third position, 98.28 points), and Uruguay (fourth position, 98.04 points) in the climate index ranking for 2021 by Numbeo (2021); and the presence of Mexico (sixth position, 6.46 points), Saudi Arabia (seventh position, 6.41 points), and Brazil (tenth position, 6.38 points) in the list of the happiest countries of the world, according to World Population Review (2021). It is obvious that these countries focus on environmental protection and harmony between society and nature allowed them to achieve notable results in the provision of well-being.

In comparison, some countries are regular outsiders in all international rankings, with low values of indicators and international statistics (without any statistical accounting or not providing data to international organizations). Without any statistical data, it is impossible to include these countries in econometric models. Accordingly, the developed solutions applied and recommendations based on these incomplete models will probably not work in these countries. Their research requires case studies and the development of recommendations for each country individually since every one of them is unique.

These are just the most obvious subcategories of emerging market economies, butmore could be distinguished during the purposeful scientific search. There is no sense in offering generalized recommendations for managing the green economy and sustainable development for emerging market economies similar to the unified developed countries. Each subcategory of developing countries needs unique recommendations The approach to managing the green economy and sustainable development in emerging market economies has to be flexible and take into account their specifics.

This turns upside down the view of the COVID-19 challenges to sustainable development and shows that the reduction took place only with certain indicators of the green economy, while its general rise was observed. Another amazing conclusion is that the COVID-19 pandemic led to an economic crisis, which became the most severe one in the past decades, but the green economy demonstrated positive dynamics. Thus the calculated reduction of GDP among emerging market economies was 7.2% on average, while the increase in green growth reached the record value of 9.8%.

The multiple examples presented demonstrate that in the face of the viral threat, the population, government, and business can unite their efforts in forming responsible communities and cities and implementing responsible production and consumption.

Numerous successful examples of implementing green innovations in emerging market economies amid the COVID-19 pandemic demonstrate the large potential of modern society in developing the green economy and supporting the implementation of the SDGs, despite the recession and deficit of financing.

On one hand, this conclusion could be interpreted as proof of deviation of the interests of economic growth and environmental protection amid the COVID-19 pandemic. This complicates much of the practical implementation of the

SDGs in emerging market economies and creates a topic for discussion. The interpretation might be the basis for scientific discussion.

On the other hand, the experience of the COVID-19 pandemic demonstrated that economic crises are not a threat to the green economy. This permits starting long-term global programmes of sustainable development, which do not depend on the cyclical character of the world economy and do not require the change of the indicators' control values and reconsideration of the terms of implementation in cases of economic crises.

The Element's contribution to literature is as follows. The theoretical significance of the study is to clarify the essence, characteristics, and concept of the green economy and sustainable development in developing countries. The practical value lies in the consideration of empirical experience and numerous examples and cases, as well as in the development of applied recommendations to improve the green economy and accelerate the sustainable development of developing countries.

In summing up the Element, it should be noted that it allows reducing uncertainty and shedding light on multiple scientific and practical aspects of the impact of the COVID-19 pandemic on the green economy and sustainable development of emerging market economies. Also, the obtained results and conclusions actualize new scientific and practical issues.

Firstly, though sustainable development envisages the balance of socio-economic and ecological interests, this balance does not mean the equality of these interests but is a preferable Pareto optimum. The balance that existed before the COVID-19 pandemic is no longer appropriate and there is a need for the search for a new balance. Thus the following question arises: which interests should dominate rapid post-crisis restoration of the economy or environment protection and support for green growth?

Secondly, the fourth industrial revolution is gaining momentum. In some areas Industry 4.0 contradicts the SDGs and in some areas it supports them. The question lies in the systemic integration of the SDGs in Industry 4.0 to develop green digital technologies. A significant head start in this direction was gained by climate-smart innovations. Still, they are connected only to SDG13, while it is necessary to cover all SDGs and perform a digital modernization of the approach to their practical implementation.

Thirdly, what are the prospects of reduction of inequality of countries? Will the COVID-19 pandemic and crisis be a reason for the final establishment of emerging market economies, or will the new context allow them to come closer to the level of developed countries in the aspect of green growth and sustainable development? This is yet to be discovered in the post-pandemic period.

Fourthly, how is it possible to ensure the systemic implementation of the SDGs that are not directly connected to environment protection and the SDGs that are based on the green economy? The origins of this question lie in the management of synergetic effect in the sphere of sustainable development, which emerges during the growth of the green economy.

Finally, will emerging market economies be able to fully implement all SDGs by 2030 or should this deadline be reconsidered? To answer this question, there is a need for a "roadmap" of the green economy and sustainable development of emerging market economies.

These questions determine the prospects of further application of scientific thought and, we hope, will be reflected in future studies.

# References

Abid, N., Ikram, M., Wu, J., Ferasso, M. (2021). Towards environmental sustainability: exploring the nexus among ISO 14001, governance indicators and green economy in Pakistan. *Sustainable Production and Consumption*, 27, 653–66. https:doi.org/10.1016/j.spc.2021.01.024

Abo Murad, M., Al-Kharabsheh, A., Al-Kharabsheh, A. (2021). Crisis management strategies in the Jordanian hotel industry. *Journal of Environmental Management and Tourism*, 12(2), 578–87. https://doi.org/10.14505//jemt.v12.2(50).27

Adnan, N., Nordin, S. M. (2021). How does COVID 19 affect the Malaysian paddy industry? Adoption of green fertilizer: a potential resolution. *Environment, Development and Sustainability*, 23(6), 8089–8129. https://doi.org/10.1007/s10668-020-00978-6

Al Asbahi, A. A. M. H., Fang, Z. G., Chandio, Z. A. et al. (2020). Assessing barriers and solutions for Yemen energy crisis to adopt green and sustainable practices: a fuzzy multi-criteria analysis. *Environmental Science and Pollution Research*, 27(29), 36765–81. https://doi.org/10.1007/s11356-020-09700-5

Ali, E. B., Anufriev, V. P., Amfo, B. (2021). Green economy implementation in Ghana as a road map for a sustainable development drive: a review. *Scientific African*, 12, e00756. https://doi.org/10.1016/j.sciaf.2021.e00756

Ali Shah, S. A., Longsheng, C., Solangi, Y.A., Ahmad, M., Ali, S. (2021). Energy trilemma based prioritization of waste-to-energy technologies: implications for post-COVID-19 green economic recovery in Pakistan. *Journal of Cleaner Production*, 28(15 February), Art. 124729. https://doi.org/10.1016/j.jclepro.2020.124729

Amnuaylojaroen, T., Parasin, N. (2021). The association between COVID-19, air pollution and climate change. *Frontiers in Public Health*, 9. https://doi.org/10.3389/fpubh.2021.662499

Arif, M., Hasan, M., Alawi, S. M., Naeem, M. A. (2021). COVID-19 and time-frequency connectedness between green and conventional financial markets. *Global Finance Journal*, 49(August): Art. 100650. https://doi.org/10.1016/j.gfj.2021.100650

Asongu, S. A., Odhiambo, N. M. (2021). The green economy and inequality in sub-Saharan Africa: avoidable thresholds and thresholds for complementary policies. *Energy Exploration and Exploitation*, 39(3), 838–52. https://doi.org/10.1177/0144598720984226

Bastida, C. E. J. L. (2020). Lessons learned and challenges that the COVID-19 pandemic is leaving us with from a green economy perspective. [Lecciones aprendidas y retos que nos esta dejando el la pandemia de covid-19 desde la visión de la economía ecológica]. *Universidad y Sociedad*, 12(3), 1–7.

Belaid, F., Ben Amar, A., Goutte, S., Guesmi, K. (2021). Emerging and advanced economies markets behaviour during the COVID-19 crisis era. *International Journal of Finance and Economics*. https://doi.org/10.1002/ijfe.2494

Belmonte-Ureña, L. J., Plaza-Úbeda, J. A., Vazquez-Brust, D., Yakovleva, N. (2021). Circular economy, degrowth and green growth as pathways for research on sustainable development goals: a global analysis and future agenda. *Ecological Economics*, 185. https://doi.org/10.1016/j.ecolecon.2021.107050

Berdejo-Espinola, V., Suárez-Castro, A. F., Amano, T., et al. (2021). Urban green space use during a time of stress: a case study during the COVID-19 pandemic in Brisbane, Australia. *People and Nature*, 3(3), 597–609. https://doi.org/10.1002/pan3.10218

Bhopal, A., Medhin, H., Bærøe, K., Norheim, O. F. (2021). Climate change and health in Ethiopia: to what extent have the health dimensions of climate change been integrated into the climate-resilient green economy?*World Medical and Health Policy*, 13(2), 293–312. https://doi.org/10.1002/wmh3.447

Bina, O. (2013). The green economy and sustainable development: an uneasy balance? *Environment and Planning C: Government and Policy*, 31(6), 1023–47. https://doi.org/10.1068/c1310j

Biswas, A., Roy, M. (2015). Green products: an exploratory study on the consumer behaviour in emerging economies of the East. *Journal of Cleaner Production*, 87(1), 463–8. https://doi.org/10.1016/j.jclepro.2014.09.075

Bocchino, A., Gilart, E., Roman, I. C., Lepiani, I. (2021). Unemployment syndrome during COVID-19: a comparison of three population groups. *International Journal of Environmental Research and Public Health*, 18(14), 7372. https://doi.org/10.3390/ijerph18147372

Borhani, F., Shafiepour Motlagh, M., Stohl, A., Rashidi, Y., Ehsani, A. H. (2021). Changes in short-lived climate pollutants during the COVID-19 pandemic in Tehran, Iran. *Environmental Monitoring and Assessment*, 193(6), 331. https://doi.org/10.1007/s10661-021-09096-w

Brady, J. (2019). How investing in the green economy is the best way to post-COVID-19 economic recovery. *Proceedings of the Institution of Civil*

*Engineers: Civil Engineering*, 173(3), 100. https://doi.org/10.1680/jcien .2020.173.3.100

Cai, G., Xu, L., Gao, W. (2021). The green B&B promotion strategies for tourist loyalty: surveying the restart of Chinese national holiday travel after COVID-19. *International Journal of Hospitality Management*, 94. https://doi.org/10 .1016/j.ijhm.2020.102704

Chae, M.-J. (2021). Effects of the COVID-19 pandemic on sustainable consumption. *Social Behavior and Personality*, 49(6), e10199. https://doi .org/10.2224/sbp.10199

Chairani, Siregar, S. V. (2021). Disclosure of enterprise risk management in ASEAN 5: Sustainable development for a green economy. *IOP Conference Series: Earth and Environmental Science*, 716(1). https://doi.org/10.1088 /1755-1315/716/1/012101

Chen, J., Huang, J., Su, W., Štreimikienė, D., Baležentis, T. (2021). The challenges of COVID-19 control policies for sustainable development of business: evidence from service industries. *Technology in Society*, 66 (August 2021), Art. 101643. https://doi.org/10.1016/j.techsoc.2021.101643

Chen, S., Golley, J. (2014). 'Green' productivity growth in China's industrial economy. *Energy Economics*, 44, 89–98. https://doi.org/10.1016/j .eneco.2014.04.002

Dabbour, L., Abdelhafez, E., Hamdan, M. (2021). Effect of climatology parameters on air pollution during COVID-19 pandemic in Jordan. *Environmental Research*, 202. https://doi.org/10.1016/j.envres.2021.111742

D'Amato, D., Droste, N., Allen, B., (. . .), Matthies, B. D. , Toppinen, A. (2017). Green, circular, bio economy: a comparative analysis of sustainability avenues. *Journal of Cleaner Production*, 168, 716–34. https://doi.org/10 .1016/j.jclepro.2017.09.053

Davidescu, A. A., Apostu, S.-A., Stoica, L. A. (2021). Socioeconomic effects of COVID-19 pandemic: exploring uncertainty in the forecast of the Romanian unemployment rate for the period 2020–2023. *Sustainability* (Switzerland), 13(13), 7078. https://doi.org/10.3390/su13137078

Dawid, H., Kort, P. M., Vergalli, S. (2021). Investments, energy, and green economy. *Journal of Economic Dynamics and Control*, 126. https://doi.org /10.1016/j.jedc.2021.104126

Dmuchowski, P., Dmuchowski, W., Baczewska-Dąbrowska, A. H., Gworek, B. (2021). Green economy: growth and maintenance of the conditions of green growth at the level of Polish local authorities. *Journal of Cleaner Production*, 301. https://doi.org/10.1016/j.jclepro.2021.126975

Escribano, A., Pena, J. (2021). *Productivity in Emerging Countries: Methodology and Firm-Level Analysis Based on International Enterprise*

*Business Surveys* (Elements in the Economics of Emerging Markets). Cambridge: Cambridge University Press. https://doi.org/10.1017 /9781108909938

Fasan, M., Soerger Zaro, E., Soerger Zaro, C., Porco, B., Tiscini, R. (2021). An empirical analysis: did green supply chain management alleviate the effects of COVID-19? *Business Strategy and the Environment*, 30(5), 2702–12. https://doi.org/10.1002/bse.2772

Fasth, J., Elliot, V., Styhre, A. (2021). Crisis management as practice in small- and medium-sized enterprises during the first period of COVID-19. *Journal of Contingencies and Crisis Management*. Wiley Online Library. https://doi .org/10.1111/1468-5973.12371

Felício, J. A., Rodrigues, R., Caldeirinha, V. (2021). Green shipping effect on sustainable economy and environmental performance. *Sustainability* (Switzerland), 13(8), 4256. https://doi.org/10.3390/su13084256

*Forbes* (2021). Top 30 ecological companies of Russia: 2020 ranking. www .forbes.ru/biznes-photogallery/422011-30-samyh-ekologichnyh-kompaniy- rossii-reyting-forbes (Accessed 26 June 2021).

Geng, R., Mansouri, S. A., Aktas, E. (2017). The relationship between green supply chain management and performance: a meta-analysis of empirical evidences in Asian emerging economies. *International Journal of Production Economics*, 183, 245–58. https://doi.org/10.1016/j.ijpe.2016.10.008

Global Green Growth Institute (2021a). GGGI Technical Report No. 5, October 2019. Green growth index: concept, methods and applications. https://greengrowthindex.gggi.org/wp-content/uploads/2019/10/ GGGI_Green_Growth_Index_report.pdf (Accessed 15 August 2021).

Global Green Growth Institute (2021b). GGGI Technical Report No. 16, December 2020. Green Growth Index 2020. Measuring performance in achieving SDG targets. https://greengrowthindex.gggi.org/wp-content /uploads/2021/01/2020-Green-Growth-Index.pdf (accessed 26 June 2021).

Goyal, S., Sergi, B. (2020). *Towards a Theory of 'Smart' Social Infrastructures at Base of the Pyramid: A Study of India* (Elements in the Economics of Emerging Markets). Cambridge: Cambridge University Press. https://doi.org /10.1017/9781108882170

Goyal, S., Sergi, B. S. (2015). Social entrepreneurship and sustainability: understanding the context and key characteristics. *Journal of Security & Sustainability*, 4(3), 269–78.

Hartono, D., Yusuf, A. A., Hastuti, S. H., Saputri, N. K., Syaifudin, N. (2021). Effect of COVID-19 on energy consumption and carbon dioxide emissions in Indonesia. *Sustainable Production and Consumption*, 28, 391–404. https:// doi.org/10.1016/j.spc.2021.06.003

Hassankhani, M., Alidadi, M., Sharifi, A., Azhdari, A. (2021). Smart city and crisis management: lessons for the COVID-19 pandemic. *International Journal of Environmental Research and Public Health*, 18(15), Art. 7736. https://doi.org/10.3390/ijerph18157736

He, R., Baležentis, T., Štreimikienė, D., Shen, Z. (2022). Sustainable green growth in developing economies: an empirical analysis on the Belt and Road countries. *Journal of Global Information Management*, 30(6). https://doi.org/10.4018/JGIM.20221101.oa1

Heynen, N., Perkins, H. A., Roy, P. (2006). The political ecology of uneven urban green space: the impact of political economy on race and ethnicity in producing environmental inequality in Milwaukee. *Urban Affairs Review*, 42(1), 3–25. https://doi.org/10.1177/1078087406290729

Ho, C.-Y., Tsai, B.-H., Chen, C.-S., Lu, M.-T. (2021). Exploring green marketing orientations toward sustainability the hospitality industry in the COVID-19 pandemic. Sustainability (Switzerland), 13(8), 4348. https://doi.org/10.3390/su13084348

Hoang, A. T., Nguyen, X. P., Le, A. T., Huynh, T. T., Pham, V. V. (2021). COVID-19 and the global shift: progress to clean energy. *Journal of Energy Resources Technology: Transactions of the ASME*, 143(9). https://doi.org/10.1115/1.4050779

Howson, P. (2021). Distributed degrowth technology: challenges for blockchain beyond the green economy. *Ecological Economics*, 184. https://doi.org/10.1016/j.ecolecon.2021.107020

Hsu, C.-C., Tan, K. C., Zailani, S. H. M., Jayaraman, V. (2013). Supply chain drivers that foster the development of green initiatives in an emerging economy. *International Journal of Operations and Production Management*, 33(6), 656–88. https://doi.org/10.1108/IJOPM-10-2011-0401

IMD (2021). World Digital Competitiveness Ranking 2020. www.imd.org/centers/world-competitiveness-center/rankings/world-digital-competitiveness (accessed 2 August 2021).

Inshakov, O. V., Bogachkova, L. Y., Popkova, E. G. (2019). Energy efficiency as a driver of global competitiveness: the priority of the state economic policy and the international collaboration of the Russian Federation. *Lecture Notes in Networks and Systems*, 44, 119–34. https://doi.org/10.1007/978-3-319-90966-0_9

Institute of Scientific Communications (2021a). Dataset: corporate social responsibility, sustainable development and the fight against climate change: imitation modelling and neural network analysis in regions of the world 2020. https://iscvolga.ru/dataset-climate-change (accessed 4 August 2021).

Institute of Scientific Communications (2021b). Dataset: social entrepreneurship in the world economy: from virtual scores to big data 2020. https://iscvolga.ru/dataset-social-predprinim (accessed 4 August 2021).

Institute of Scientific Communications (2021c). Dataset: big data of the modern world economy: a digital platform for intellectual analytics 2020. https://iscvolga.ru/dataset1-bolshie-dannie (accessed 4 August 2021).

Institute of Scientific Communications (2021d). Dataset: COVID-19 and the 2020 crisis: capabilities of healthcare and the consequences for economy and business around the world. https://iscvolga.ru/dataset-crisis-2020 (accessed 2 August 2021).

International Monetary Fund (2021). World economic outlook database by countries April 2021. www.imf.org/en/Publications/WEO/weo-database/2021/April (accessed 2 August 2021).

Iyengar, K. P., Jain, V. K., Kariya, A. D. (2021). Planning and analysing 'green' post-COVID-19 orthopaedic perioperative recovery pathway. *Journal of Perioperative Practice*, 31(4),147–52. https://doi.org/10.1177/1750458921993361

Jiang, P., Klemeš, J. J., Fan, Y. V., et al. (2021). Energy, environmental, economic and social equity (4E) pressures of COVID-19 vaccination mismanagement: a global perspective. *Energy*, 235. https://doi.org/10.1016/j.energy.2021.121315

Jin, M., Zhang, X., Xiong, Y., Zhou, Y. (2021). Implications of green optimism upon sustainable supply chain management. *European Journal of Operational Research*, 295(1): 131–9. https://doi.org/10.1016/j.ejor.2021.02.036

Kaklauskas, A., Lepkova, N., Raslanas, S., et al. (2021). COVID-19 and green housing: a review of relevant literature. *Energies*, 14(8), 2072. https://doi.org/10.3390/en14082072

Kalikov, M., Uteyev, B. Z., Khajieva, A., Torekulova, U. A. (2020). Green economy as a paradigm of sustainable development of the Republic of Kazakhstan. *Journal of Environmental Accounting and Management*, 8(3), 281–92. https://doi.org/10.5890/JEAM.2020.09.006

Karmaker, C. L., Ahmed, T., Ahmed, S. et al. (2021). Improving supply chain sustainability in the context of COVID-19 pandemic in an emerging economy: exploring drivers using an integrated model. *Sustainable Production and Consumption*, 26, 411–27. https://doi.org/10.1016/j.spc.2020.09.019

Kuzmynchuk, N., Kutsenko, T., Zyma, O., Terovanesova, O., Bachkir, I. (2021). Paradigm Towards ensuring energy saving in the crisis management conditions in the aspect of sustainable environmental development. *E3S Web of Conferences*, 255(2021), Art. 01022:1–7. https://doi.org/10.1051/e3sconf/202125501022

Lahcen, B., Brusselaers, J., Vrancken, K., et al. (2020). Green recovery policies for the COVID-19 crisis: modelling the impact on the economy and greenhouse gas emissions. *Environmental and Resource Economics*, 76(4), 731–50. https://doi.org/10.1007/s10640-020-00454-9

Lazzini, S., Occhipinti, Z., Parenti, A., Verona, R. (2021). Disentangling economic crisis effects from environmental regulation effects: implications for sustainable development. *Business Strategy and the Environment*, 30(5), 2332–53. https://doi.org/10.1002/bse.2749

Leal Filho, W., Wall, T., Alves, F., et al. (2021). The impacts of the early outset of the COVID-19 pandemic on climate change research: implications for policy-making. *Environmental Science and Policy*, 124, 267–78. https://doi.org/10.1016/j.envsci.2021.06.008

Liu, R., Gao, Z., Nayga, R. M., et al. (2020). Can 'green food' certification achieve both sustainable practices and economic benefits in a transitional economy? The case of kiwifruit growers in Henan Province, China. *Agribusiness*, 36(4), 675–92. https://doi.org/10.1002/agr.21641

Liu, Y., Dong, F. (2021). How technological innovation impacts urban green economy efficiency in emerging economies: a case study of 278 Chinese cities. *Resources, Conservation and Recycling*, 169. https://doi.org/10.1016/j.resconrec.2021.105534

Liu, Z., Liu, T., Liu, X. et al. (2021). Research on optimization of healthcare waste management system based on green governance principle in the COVID-19 pandemic. *International Journal of Environmental Research and Public Health*, 18(10), 5316. https://doi.org/10.3390/ijerph18105316

Loiseau, E., Saikku, L., Antikainen, et al. (2016). Green economy and related concepts: an overview. *Journal of Cleaner Production*, 139, 361–71. https://doi.org/10.1016/j.jclepro.2016.08.024

Lorek, S., Spangenberg, J. H. (2014). Sustainable consumption within a sustainable economy: beyond green growth and green economies. *Journal of Cleaner Production*, 63, 33–44. https://doi.org/10.1016/j.jclepro.2013.08.045

Lovejoy, T. E. (2021). Nature, COVID-19, disease prevention and climate change. *Biological Conservation*, 261. https://doi.org/10.1016/j.biocon.2021.109213

MacGregor Pelikanova, R., Cvik, E. D., MacGregor, R. K. (2021). Addressing the COVID-19 challenges by SMEs in the hotel industry: a Czech sustainability message for emerging economies. *Journal of Entrepreneurship in Emerging Economies*. https://doi.org/10.1108/JEEE-07-2020-0245

Madineni, V. R., Dasari, H. P., Karumuri, R. et al. (2021). Natural processes dominate the pollution levels during the COVID-19 lockdown over India. *Scientific Reports*, 11(1). https://doi.org/10.1038/s41598-021-94373-4

Matousek, R., Rummel, O. (2020). *Cross-Border Interbank Contagion Risk Analysis: Evidence from Selected Emerging and Less-Developed Economies in the Asia-Pacific Region.* Elements in the Economics of Emerging Markets. Cambridge: Cambridge University Press. https://doi.org/10.1017/9781108882040

Mayen Huerta, C., Utomo, A. (2021). Evaluating the association between urban green spaces and subjective well-being in Mexico city during the COVID-19 pandemic. *Health and Place*, 70. https://doi.org/10.1016/j.healthplace.2021.102606

Mayen Huerta, C., Cafagna, G. (2021). Snapshot of the use of urban green spaces in Mexico City during the COVID-19 pandemic: a qualitative study. *International Journal of Environmental Research and Public Health*, 18(8), 4304. https://doi.org/10.3390/ijerph18084304

Mell, I., Whitten, M. (2021). Access to nature in a post-COVID-19 world: opportunities for green infrastructure financing, distribution and equitability in urban planning. *International Journal of Environmental Research and Public Health*, 18(4),1527, 1–16. https://doi.org/10.3390/ijerph18041527

Mikhno, I., Koval, V., Shvets, G., Garmatiuk, O., Tamošiūnienė, R. (2021). Green economy in sustainable development and improvement of resource efficiency. *Central European Business Review*, 10(1), 99–113. https://doi.org/10.18267/j.cebr.252

Mitman, K., Rabinovich, S. (2021). Whether, when and how to extend unemployment benefits: theory and application to COVID-19. *Journal of Public Economics*, 200. https://doi.org/10.1016/j.jpubeco.2021.104447

Mo, Z., Huang, J., Chen, Z. et al. (2021). Cause analysis of PM2.5 pollution during the COVID-19 lockdown in Nanning, China. *Scientific Reports*, 11(1). https://doi.org/10.1038/s41598-021-90617-5

Mohideen, M. M., Ramakrishna, S., Prabu, S., Liu, Y. (2021). Advancing green energy solutions with the impetus of the COVID-19 pandemic. *Journal of Energy Chemistry*, 59, 688–705. https://doi.org/10.1016/j.jechem.2020.12.005

Mondejar, M. E., Avtar, R., Diaz, H. L. B. et al. (2021). Digitalization to achieve sustainable development goals: steps towards a smart green planet. *Science of the Total Environment*, 794. https://doi.org/10.1016/j.scitotenv.2021.148539

Naeem, M. A., Farid, S., Ferrer, R., Shahzad, S. J. H. (2021a). Comparative efficiency of green and conventional bonds pre- and during COVID-19: an asymmetric multifractal detrended fluctuation analysis. *Energy Policy*, 153. https://doi.org/10.1016/j.enpol.2021.112285

Naeem, M. A., Mbarki, I., Alharthi, M., Omri, A., Shahzad, S. J. H. (2021b). Did COVID-19 impact the connectedness between green Bonds and other financial markets? Evidence from the time–frequency domain with portfolio implications. *Frontiers in Environmental Science*, 9. https://doi.org/10.3389/fenvs.2021.657533

Nam, H., Nam, T. (2021). Exploring strategic directions of pandemic crisis management: a text analysis of World Economic Forum COVID-19 reports. *Sustainability* (Switzerland), 13(8), Art. 4123. https://doi.org/10.3390/su13084123

National Research University Higher School of Economics. (2021). Goroda posle pandemii: kak obespechit' ustoychivoe razvitie v novykh usloviyakh [Cities after the pandemic: ensuring sustainable development in new conditions]. www.hse.ru/news/community/444777162.html (accessed 4 August 2021).

Negev, M., Dahdal, Y., Khreis, H. et al. (2021). Regional lessons from the COVID-19 outbreak in the Middle East: from infectious diseases to climate change adaptation. *Science of the Total Environment*, 768. https://doi.org/10.1016/j.scitotenv.2020.144434

Numbeo (2021). Quality of life index by country 2021 mid-year. www.numbeo.com/quality-of-life/rankings_by_country.jsp (accessed 18 August 2021).

Nundy, S., Ghosh, A., Mesloub, A., Albaqawy, G. A., Alnaim, M. M. (2021). Impact of the COVID-19 pandemic on socio-economic, energy-environment and transport sectors globally and Sustainable Development Goal (SDG). *Journal of Cleaner Production*, 312. https://doi.org/10.1016/j.jclepro.2021.127705

Odugbesan, J. A., Rjoub, H., Ifediora, C. U., Iloka, C. B. (2021). Do financial regulations matter for a sustainable green economy? Evidence from Turkey. *Environmental Science and Pollution Research*. https://doi.org/10.1007/s11356-021-14645-4

Our World in Data. (2021). Share of people vaccinated against COVID-19. https://ourworldindata.org/covid-vaccinations?country=OWID_WRL (accessed 2 August 2021).

Pan, J., Bardhan, R., Jin, Y. (2021). Spatial distributive effects of public green space and COVID-19 infection in London. *Urban Forestry and Urban Greening*, 62. https://doi.org/10.1016/j.ufug.2021.127182

Pereira, M. M. O., Silva, M. E., Hendry, L. C. (2021). Supply chain sustainability learning: the COVID-19 impact on emerging economy suppliers. *Supply Chain Management*. https://doi.org/10.1108/SCM-08-2020-0407

Ponte, S. (2008). Greener than thou: the political economy of fish ecolabeling and its local manifestations in South Africa. *World Development*, 36(1), 159–75. https://doi.org/10.1016/j.worlddev.2007.02.014

Popkova, E., Bogoviz, A. V., Sergi, B. S. (2021). Towards digital society management and 'capitalism 4.0' in contemporary Russia. *Humanities and Social Sciences Communications*, 8(77). https://doi.org/10.1057/s41599-021-00743-8

Popkova, E. G., DeLo, O., Sergi, B. S. (2020). Corporate social responsibility amid social distancing during the COVID-19 crisis: BRICS vs. OECD countries. *Research in International Business and Finance*, 55, Art. 10135. https://doi.org/10.1016/j.ribaf.2020.101315

Popkova, E. G., Inshakov, O. V., Bogoviz, A. V. (2019). Regulatory mechanisms of energy conservation in sustainable economic development. *Lecture Notes in Networks and Systems*, 44, 107–18. https://doi.org/10.1007/978-3-319-90966-0_8

Popkova, E. G., Sergi, B. S. (2020a). Energy efficiency in leading emerging and developed countries. *Energy*, 221(1). https://doi.org/10.1016/j.energy.2020.119730

Popkova, E. G., Sergi, B. S. (2020b). Social entrepreneurship in Russia and Asia: further development trends and prospects. *On the Horizon*, 28(1), 9–21. https://doi.org/10.1108/OTH-09-2019-0065

Popkova, E. G., Sergi, B. S. (2020c). Human capital and AI in industry 4.0: convergence and divergence in social entrepreneurship in Russia. *Journal of Intellectual Capital*, 21(4),565–81. https://doi.org/10.1108/JIC-09-2019-0224

Popkova, E. G., Sergi, B. S. (2020d). Digital public health: automation based on new datasets and the Internet of Things. *Socio-economic Planning Sciences*, 2021, 101039. https://doi.org/10.1016/j.seps.2021.101039

Popkova, E. G., Sergi, B. S. (2021). Paths to the development of social entrepreneurship in Russia and Central Asian countries: standardization versus deregulation. In *Entrepreneurship for Social Change*, 161–77. Bingley, UK: Emerald. https://doi.org/10.1108/978-1-80071-210-220211006

Prakash, N., Sethi, M. (2021). Green bonds driving sustainable transition in Asian economies: the case of India. *Journal of Asian Finance, Economics and Business*, 8(1),723–32. https://doi.org/10.13106/jafeb.2021.vol8.no1.723

Rita, E., Chizoo, E., Cyril, U. S. (2021). Sustaining COVID-19 pandemic lockdown era air pollution impact through the utilization of more renewable energy resources. *Heliyon*, 7(7), e07455. https://doi.org/10.1016/j.heliyon.2021.e07455

Rosbusinessconsulting (RBC). (2021). Vzryvnoy rost: glavnoe iz otcheta po ustoychivomu razvitiyu biznesa v Rossii. [Explosive growth: the main points of the report on sustainable development of business in Russia]. https://trends .rbc.ru/trends/green/60dafb1f9a7947736717b374 (accessed 4 August 2021).

Sardar, T., Jianqiu, Z., Bilal, M., Syed, N. (2021). Impact of ICT on entrepreneurial self-efficacy in an emerging economy: sustaining lockdown during the COVID-19 pandemic. *Human Systems Management*, 40(2), 299–314. https://doi.org/10.3233/HSM-201066

Sergi, B. S., Popkova, E. G., Borzenko, K. V., Przhedetskaya, N. V. (2019). Public-private partnerships as a mechanism of financing sustainable development. In Ziolo, Magdalena and Bruno S. Sergi (eds.), *Financing Sustainable Development: Key Challenges and Prospects* (pp. 313–39). Palgrave Macmillan.

Sharma, R. R. (2020). Green management and circular economy for sustainable development. *Vision*, 24(1), 7–8. https://doi.org/10.1177/09722629 20912497

Sosa, L., Pereira, C. (2020). *Exchange Rates in South America's Emerging Markets*. Elements in the Economics of Emerging Markets. Cambridge: Cambridge University Press. https://doi.org/10.1017/9781108893671

Spano, G., D'Este, M., Giannico, V., et al. (2021). Association between indoor-outdoor green features and psychological health during the COVID-19 lockdown in Italy: a cross-sectional nationwide study. *Urban Forestry and Urban Greening*, 62. https://doi.org/10.1016/j .ufug.2021.127156

Sriyono, B., Proyogi, B. (2021). Acceleration of performance recovery and competitiveness through non-banking financing in SMEs based on the green economy: impact of the Covid-19 pandemic. *Journal of Innovation and Entrepreneurship*, 10(1), 27. https://doi.org/10.1186/s13731-021-00166-4

Stanley, L. (2020). *Latin America Global Insertion, Energy Transition, and Sustainable Development*. Elements in the Economics of Emerging Markets. Cambridge: Cambridge University Press. https://doi.org/10.1017 /9781108893398

StartupBlink, UNAIDS (2021). Global rankings of cities on coronavirus innovation. https://coronavirus.startupblink.com (accessed 2 August 2021).

Sun, X., Su, W., Guo, X., Tian, Z. (2021). The impact of awe induced by the COVID-19 pandemic on green consumption behaviour in China. *International Journal of Environmental Research and Public Health*, 18(2), 543. https://doi.org/10.3390/ijerph18020543

Svabova, L., Tesarova, E. N., Durica, M., Strakova, L. (2021). Evaluation of the impacts of the COVID-19 pandemic on the development of the unemployment rate in Slovakia: counterfactual before-after comparison. *Equilibrium: Quarterly Journal of Economics and Economic Policy*, 16(2), 261–84. https://doi.org/10.24136/eq.2021.010

Taghizadeh-Hesary, F., Yoshino, N., Phoumin, H. (2021). Analyzing the characteristics of green bond markets to facilitate green finance in the post–COVID-19 world. *Sustainability* (Switzerland), 13(10), 5719. https://doi.org/10.3390/su13105719

Ullah, H., Wang, Z., Bashir, S., et al. (2021). Nexus between IT capability and green intellectual capital on sustainable businesses: evidence from emerging economies. *Environmental Science and Pollution Research*, 28(22), 27825–43. https://doi.org/10.1007/s11356-020-12245-2

United Nations Development Programme (UNDP) (2021). Sustainable development report 2020: SDG index ranking. https://dashboards.sdgindex.org/rankings (accessed 2 August 2021).

Vasquez-Apestegui, B. V., Parras-Garrido, E., Tapia, V. et al. (2021). Association between air pollution in Lima and the high incidence of COVID-19: findings from a post hoc Analysis. *BMC Public Health*, 21(1). https://doi.org/10.1186/s12889-021-11232-7

Venter, Z. S., Barton, D. N., Gundersen, V., Figari, H., Nowell, M. S. (2021). Back to nature: Norwegians sustain increased recreational use of urban green space months after the COVID-19 outbreak. *Landscape and Urban Planning*, 214(October 2020), Art. 104175. https://doi.org/10.1016/j.landurbplan.2021.104175

Vijay, V., Karakunnel, J. J., Loganathan, S., Meyer, D. F. (2021). From a recession to the COVID-19 pandemic: inflation–unemployment comparison between the UK and India. *Economies*, 9(2): 73. https://doi.org/10.3390/economies9020073

Wamboye, E. (2021). *China's Finance in Africa: What and How Much?* Elements in the Economics of Emerging Markets. Cambridge: Cambridge University Press. https://doi.org/10.1017/9781108893350

Wang, Q., Huang, R. (2021). The impact of the COVID-19 pandemic on sustainable development goals: a survey. *Environmental Research*, 202 (November 2020), Art. 111637. https://doi.org/10.1016/j.envres.2021.111637

Wang, Q., Li, S., Jiang, F. (2021). Uncovering the impact of the COVID-19 pandemic on energy consumption: new insight from the difference between pandemic-free scenario and actual electricity consumption in China. *Journal of Cleaner Production*, 313. https://doi.org/10.1016/j.jclepro.2021.127897

Wang, Y., Lei, X., Zhao, D., Long, R., Wu, M. (2021). The dual impacts of green credit on economy and environment: evidence from China. *Sustainability* (Switzerland), 13(8), 4574. https://doi.org/10.3390/su13084574

Wodak, R. (2021). Crisis communication and crisis management during COVID-19. *Global Discourse*, 11(3), 329–53. https://doi.org/10.1332/204378921X16100431230102

World Economic Forum (WEF). (2021). Global competitiveness report special edition 2020: how countries are performing on the road to recovery. www.weforum.org/reports/the-global-competitiveness-report-2020 (accessed 2 August 2021).

World Energy Council (2021). World energy trilemma index 2020 report. https://trilemma.worldenergy.org (accessed 4 August 2021).

World Health Organization (WHO). (2021). WHO coronavirus (COVID-19) dashboard. https://covid19.who.int/?gclid=Cj0KCQjwrIf3BRD1ARIsAMu ugNsIqvkZsmIoto8RJ964Wv1YdYllaCbKloYu2Z9HLeUkZuatNROZyzga AvEiEALw_wcB (accessed 2 August 2021).

World Population Review (2021). Happiest countries in the world 2021. https://worldpopulationreview.com/country-rankings/happiest-countries-in-the-world (accessed 18 August 2021).

Ye, T., Guo, S., Xie, Y. et al. (2021). Health and related economic benefits associated with a reduction in air pollution during the COVID-19 outbreak in 367 Cities in China. *Ecotoxicology and Environmental Safety*, 222. https://doi.org/10.1016/j.ecoenv.2021.112481

Ying, L., Li, M., Yang, J. (2021). Agglomeration and driving factors of regional innovation space based on intelligent manufacturing and green economy. *Environmental Technology and Innovation*, 22. https://doi.org/10.1016/j.eti.2021.101398

Zhao, M., Liu, F., Song, Y., Geng, J. (2020). Impact of air pollution regulation and technological investment on sustainable development of green economy in eastern China: empirical analysis with panel data approach. *Sustainability* (Switzerland), 12(8), 3073. https://doi.org/10.3390/SU12083073

# Acknowledgement

I would like to express my sincere thanks and appreciation to Prof. Bruno S. Sergi for many years of cooperation, professional help, friendly participation, productive work, and great support.

## Cambridge Elements ≡

# Economics of Emerging Markets

## Bruno S. Sergi
*Harvard University*

Editor Bruno S. Sergi is an instructor at Harvard University and an associate of the Harvard University Davis Center for Russian and Eurasian Studies and the Harvard Ukrainian Research Institute. He is the academic series editor of the Cambridge Elements in the Economics of Emerging Markets (Cambridge University Press), a co-editor of the *Lab for Entrepreneurship and Development* book series, and an associate editor of *The American Economist*. Concurrently, he teaches international economics at the University of Messina and is the scientific director of the Lab for Entrepreneurship and Development (LEAD) and a co-founder and scientific director of the International Center for Emerging Markets Research at RUDN University in Moscow. He has published more than 150 articles in professional journals and twenty-one books as author, co-author, editor, and co-editor.

## About the Series

The aim of this Elements series is to deliver state-of-the-art, comprehensive coverage of the knowledge developed to date, including the dynamics and prospects of these economies, focusing on emerging markets' economics, finance, banking, technology advances, trade, demographic challenges, and their economic relations with the rest of the world, as well as the causal factors and limits of economic policy in these markets.

# Cambridge Elements $\equiv$

## Economics of Emerging Markets

### Elements in the Series

*Towards a Theory of "Smart" Social Infrastructures at Base of the Pyramid: A Study of India*
Sandeep Goyal and Bruno S. Sergi

*Exchange Rates in South America's Emerging Markets*
Luis Molinas Sosa and Caio Vigo Pereira

*Cross-Border Interbank Contagion Risk Analysis: Evidence from Selected Emerging and Less-Developed Economies in the Asia-Pacific Region*
Roman Matousek and Ole Rummel

*Latin America Global Insertion, Energy Transition, and Sustainable Development*
Leonardo E. Stanley

*China's Finance in Africa: What and How Much?*
Evelyn F. Wamboye

*Productivity in Emerging Countries: Methodology and Firm-Level Analysis Based on International Enterprise Business Surveys*
Alvaro Escribano and Jorge Pena

*Diagnosing Human Capital As a Binding Constraint to Growth: Tests, Symptoms and Prescriptions*
Miguel Angel Santos and Farah Hani

*The Economics of Digital Shopping in Central and Eastern Europe*
Barbara Grabiwoda and Bogdan Mróz

*Can BRICS De-dollarize the Global Financial System?*
Zongyuan Zoe Liu and Mihaela Papa

*Advanced Issues in the Green Economy and Sustainable Development in Emerging Market Economies*
Elena G. Popkova

A full series listing is available at: www.cambridge.org/EEM

Printed in the United States
by Baker & Taylor Publisher Services